Text Book of Mechanical Drawing ...

Anonymous

Introduction.

The purpose of this book is to aid pupils in the study of the principles under-lying mechanical drawing. It is not intended to make the study easy, for the pupil cannot be benefited in that way. For that reason, though the drawings are made sufficiently accurate to serve as illustrations of the text, they are not so accurate or complete as to permit their use as flat studies to be merely copied without disclosing the copyist's ignorance of the principles intended to be taught. Nor are the ex-planations made so full and complete as to relieve the pupil of the necessity of thinking. In short, this book by its text and illustrations, will enable the earnest pupil to study the art and get a firm grasp upon the principles of projection, but it will be of no use to the careless pupil who seeks to skim over his studies and make nothing more than a show of understanding.

The subject is presented in a way that is likely to be interesting, and the problems set are of great practical value. The study is not an easy one—if it were it would be of less value than it is—but those who give it serious attention will soon find that what at first seemed hard to understand has become quite simple, and that they have been prepared by a thorough mastery of principles to understand and make the most complex mechanical drawings. This is the end in view. Copy-ing from flat drawings is useful only as an exercise with the pen and other instru-ments; the mastery of the principles of projection gives the pupil the key to original work.

JOHN S. ROOKE.

Philadelphia, September 1902.

Orthographic Projection.

Our first illustration is intended to show what is meant by orthographic projection ; the pupil will hereafter have to imagine these planes represented by glass.

In Fig. h we have a rectangular prism placed within a case of plates of glass upon which the projections of the prism are made. These plates of glass represent the planes of projection, and can be revolved about the axes a b and b c, until all are in one plane as in Fig. b, which is called the plane of the paper. h^h is called the horizontal plane, a^v the front vertical, and c^v the side vertical. Suppose c^v to be revolved about b c until it is in the same plane as a^v, and that c^v and a^v are revolved about a b until they are in the same plane as h^h, then we have Fig. b.

The projections from all points of an object perpendicular to these planes of projection are called orthographic projections. The projection on h^h is called the top or plan, on a^v the front elevation, and on c^v the side elevation. It can readily be seen without any reference to the planes that these views are arranged as common sense would suggest, bringing the top to the top, the front to the front, and the side to the side.

In the illustrations the small letters h and v are used with all other letters to indicate in one case the horizontal and in the other the vertical planes.

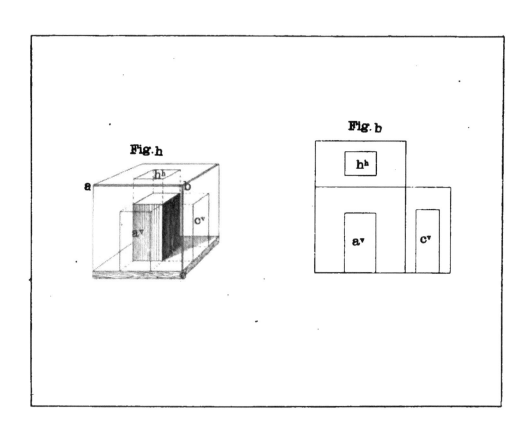

Fig. h

Fig. b

Conventional Shade Lines.

The light is assumed to come from the upper left hand corner of the drawing at an angle of 45 degrees to all horizontal and vertical lines.

This method is very simple and easy to remember, inasmuch, as in every view of the drawing of an object, the bottom and right-hand side of each plane surface which is visible are shade lines.

These lines always lie between the arrows which are drawn parallel to the 45-degree line.

Fig. A.—This is an illustration of external shading of a cylinder. Draw the circle, then, with the same radius, and a point on the 45-degree line as a center, and about $\frac{1}{100}$ or $\frac{1}{64}$ of an inch from the original center, draw a semi-circle which will give the desired shading.

Note.—This center should be on that part of the 45-degree line that lies between the original center and the upper left-hand corner of the drawing, for external and internal shading.

Fig. B.—This is an illustration of internal shading of a cylinder, and is done in the same manner as the cylinder in Fig. A.

Fig. C.—This is an illustration of external shading of a prism of 4 sides when two of the sides are parallel to the 45-degree line.

Fig. D.—This is an illustration of external shading of a prism of 4 sides when a diagonal of the prism is parallel to the 45-degree line.

Fig. E.—This is an illustration of external shading when one view shows two, or more dimensions. A cylinder should be shaded in like manner.

Fig. F.—This is an end view of Fig. E, and illustrates external shading. The inner polygon represents the extension on the right of Fig. E. Cylinders are shaded in like manner.

Fig. G.—This is an illustration of external shading of a prism. Cylinders are shaded in the same manner.

Fig. H.—This is an end view of Fig. G, and illustrates external and internal shading. The outer polygon illustrates the external, and the inner polygon the internal shading ; the latter being an end view of the hole shown in Fig. G by the dotted outline. The same rule is applied to cylinders.

Fig. I.—This is an illustration of external and internal shading of a hexagonal prism when two of the sides are parallel to the vertical plane.

The outer polygon illustrates the external, and the inner polygon the internal shading, and signifies that the surface of the inner polygon is below the surface of the outer polygon, or a hole the entire length of the prism.

Fig. J.—This is an illustration of external shading of a hexagonal prism when two of the sides are parallel to the front vertical plane. The inner polygon illustrates a surface that is above the surface of the outer polygon.

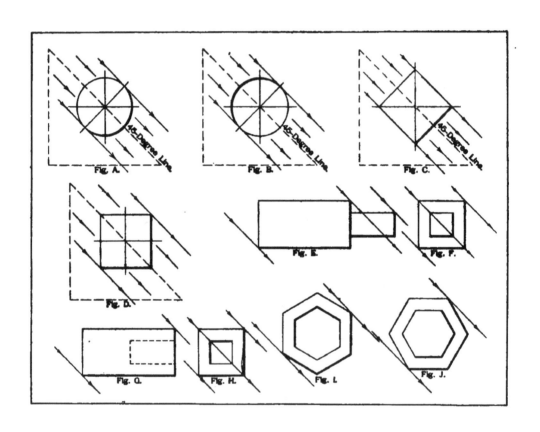

Fig. A.   45-Degree Line

Fig. B.   45-Degree Line

Fig. C.   45-Degree Line

Fig. D.

Fig. E.

Fig. F.

Fig. G.

Fig. H.

Fig. I.

Fig. J.

Drawing Instruments.

Compass.—The compass, as shown, is used for drawing circles and arcs of circles in pencil or ink. It should always be opened and closed with one hand, nor should both hands be used to place the needle point at a point on the drawing.

A pen is provided for drawing circles in ink, which fits into the same socket as the pencil holder B.

In drawing circles, the compass should be handled by the upper portion with as .ittle pressure as possible; as the weight of the instrument is sufficient to keep the needle point in the paper.

The points should always be kept perpendicular to the paper, especially when drawing circles in ink, therefore each leg is jointed as shown at B and C.

The needle point F, has a square shoulder at the lower end from which a fine points projects as shown in the figure; this shoulder will resist any reasonable pressure, and is intended to prevent large holes from being made in the paper.

The lengthening bar is used for drawing circles of large radii, and fits into the same socket as the pencil holder.

The Hair-Spring Divider.—This instrument is used for dividing lines or circles into any number of equal parts, also, for transferring distances.

When in use it should be held between the thumb and index-finger and rotated in opposite directions.

The alternate movements will cause it to remain between the thumb and finger.

The lower part of the leg, on the right of the illustration, is attached to a steel spring, which is fitted into a groove in the upper part of the leg, and secured to it at the upper end of the groove.

The lower end of the spring is drilled and tapped to receive a small thumb-screw, as shown. The spring is so arranged, that if the thumb-screw be turned from right to left, this leg will move toward the other leg, thereby, decreasing the distance between the legs.

This arrangement gives to the point a very refined adjustment, which makes it very useful for spacing gear teeth, and any work, where great accuracy is required.

The Ruling Pen.—This pen, as shown in the figure, is used for inking in lines other than circles or arcs of circles after they have been drawn with the pencil, and should be held as nearly perpendicular to the paper as possible, with the axis of the adjusting screw D, perpendicular to the edge of the T-square, or whatever may be used for a guide, and the third and fourth fingers resting upon and moving along the guide toward the right.

If the pen is held so that the point of one blade touches the paper, lines that are ragged on one edge will be the result. If it is held so that both points touch the paper, and is in good condition, lines that are smooth and clean-cut on both edges will be produced.

Bow Divider.—The bow divider is used for spacing and transferring distances of 1 inch and less.

Bow Compass.—The bow compass is used for drawing circles or arcs of circles in pencil, whose radii are 1 inch and less.

The Bow Pen.—The bow pen is used for inking in circles and arcs of circles whose radii are 1 inch and less.

Beam Compass.—The beam compass is an instrument for drawing circles and arcs of circles, in pencil or ink, of radii that exceeds the range of the compass heretofore described.

This compass consists of a wooden bar and two metal heads which can be clamped to the bar at any point in its length.

One of these heads is provided with a pencil holder and pen, and the other with a needle point.

After the heads have been set as close as may be to the required radius, the final and exact adjustment is made by the nut H.

8

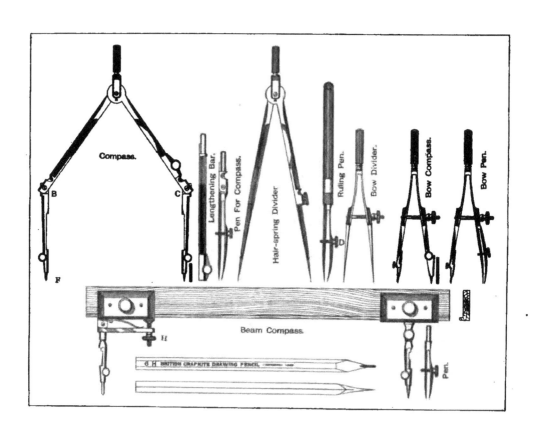

Drawing Board and Triangles.

One of the two triangles in most general use has two angles of 45 degrees each, and one of 90 degrees, right angle, and is known as the 45–degree triangle.

The other triangle is known as the 30 x 60–degree triangle, and has one angle of 30 degrees, one of 60 degrees and one of 90 degrees, right angle.

Triangles may be used to draw lines that are parallel to each other. Place any edge of triangle B so as to coincide with a given line, or points, and bring the edge, of greatest length, of triangle A into contact with one edge of B as shown ; hold A stationary and slide B upon A.

To draw a parallelogram or any similar figure. Place the edge, most suitable, so as to coincide with a given line, or points, and bring the edge, of greatest length, of C in contact with D ; hold C stationary and slide D upon C. Use the upper edge of D for the long lines and the right-hand edge for the short lines.

· To obtain 15 degrees. Bring the head of the T-square in perfect contact with the edge of the drawing board ; bring the lower edge of triangle E in contact with the edge of the T–square and place F as shown.

The 45–degree triangle is shown in position for drawing lines at an angle of 45 degrees.

Place the 30x60 degree triangle in the position shown to draw vertical lines, and lines that are at an angle of 60 degrees to the edge of the T–square and 30 degrees to a perpendicular.

General Instruction.

The drawings should be made on sheets of paper 17 x 22 inches with margin lines ½ inch from the edge of the paper, which will make the measurement inside the margin lines 16 x 21 inches. The paper should be fastened on the drawing board with thumb tacks. One in each corner will be sufficient, care being taken to have the paper put on the board square, and as tightly stretched as possible.

The T square should be used with the head against the left edge of the drawing board (unless the person is left-handed) and the pencil be sharpened to a flat point, similar to a thin wedge, and always kept sharp. The pencil for the compass must be sharpened in the same way.

The drawing and compass pens must also be kept sharp and perfectly clean. Never lay them down or put them away without first cleaning them. A small piece of chamois is very good for this purpose.

All horizontal lines should be drawn with the T square, and all vertical lines with the triangle set against the upper edge of the T square.

All drawings should be made in pencil first, with as much care as though they were not to be inked. If a drawing is not penciled accurately and neatly, it cannot be expected to be neat after it is inked. Do not leave superfluous lead pencil lines on the drawing, but erase all except those to be inked.

The drawing having been finished in pencil, proceed to ink in. Fill the drawing pen with ink; then on a small piece of paper, the same as that used for the drawing, try the pen until it makes such a line as is desirable for the work. Then with the straight edge about $\frac{1}{32}$ inch from the pencil line on the drawing, proceed with the inking, holding the pen as nearly perpendicular to the paper as possible. The pen should always be tested on the extra piece of paper, after filling, before it is used on the drawing.

All lines forming the object should be black; all construction and dimension lines, fine red. These red lines are shown on the plates by two dots and one dash, but on the drawings they are to be full lines. The center lines should be fine blue lines. They are shown on the plates by one dot and dash, but on the drawings are to be full lines. Any part of the object outside of a cutting plane will be drawn with a long and short black dot.

All arcs should be inked first, as it is easier to draw a straight line to an arc, than to draw an arc to a straight line.

All figures and arrow points should be made in black ink with a fine writing pen. An Esterbrook, No. 1170, is a good pen for this work, or a Gillott, No. 303.

The shape of a draughtsman's scale is such that when it is laid on the paper, the lines forming the divisions of the scale will come down to the paper, which enables the draughtsman to mark the dimensions directly from the scale. Dimensions may thus be marked off more quickly and accurately than by setting the dividers to the scale, and besides that the scale is thus preserved from being injured by the sharp points of the instruments.

Plate 1.

Fig. 1 represents full black lines to be drawn ¼ inch apart. The pupil will be careful to draw them off accurately and ink in carefully.

Fig. 2 represents full black lines to be drawn to the measurements given, using care to have them accurate.

Fig. 3 represents lines which the pupil will lay off to the measurements given. The first three lines represent a fine black line as used in drawing. The next three lines show how fine a red or blue line should be drawn. The first and last of the three should be drawn in red, and the middle one in blue. The next three lines represent shade lines, and should be drawn in black. The next three represent a fine black dotted line. The next three represent long and short dotted lines, and will be used to indicate parts of a figure which are cut off.

Fig. 4 is an exercise in section lining to represent cast iron, and is to be drawn in black.

Fig. 5 represents wrought iron. The section lining is to be in blue, three lines being drawn then a space left, followed by three more lines and a space, and so on until the drawing has been finished.

Fig. 6 represents steel. It is to be in blue, and drawn like Fig. 5, except that the middle line should be dotted.

Fig. 7 represents brass, and the section lining is to be done in red, with two lines instead of three, and a space.

The lines forming the outlines of all of these figures will be in black ink.

Plate .1

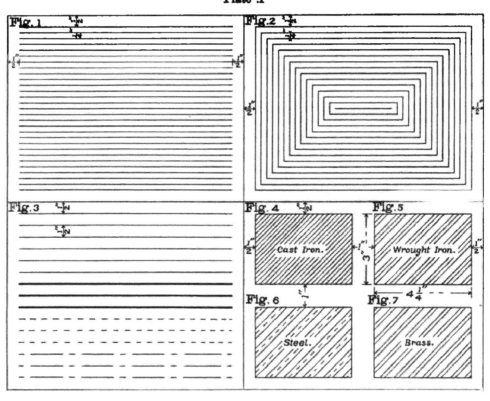

Plate 2.

Fig. 8. To bisect a straight line. Let a b be the straight line; then with **a** and b as centers, and any radius greater than one-half of a b, draw the two arcs c and d. A line through c and d will bisect a b.

Fig. 9. To bisect an arc of a circle a b c. Join a c with a straight line, and proceed as in Fig. 8.

Fig. 10. To draw a tangent to the arc of a circle when the center is not accessible. Let a be the given point upon the given arc d a c. Lay off equal distances upon the arc from a to c and to d. Join c and d. From d as a center, and radius d a draw arc a g; then with the same radius and **a** as a center, draw arcs d b, c e. Then make d b and c e equal in length to g a. A straight line through the points thus found will be tangent to a.

Fig. 11. To erect a perpendicular to a line a b from a point a or near its end. With **a** as a center and any radius, draw the arc d c. With d as a center and the same radius cut d c in c. With c as a center and the same radius, draw an arc over a. Then draw a line through d and c, producing it to intersect the last arc in e. A line from a to e will be the perpendicular.

Fig. 12. To divide a straight line a b into any number of equal parts, say four. Draw a c at any angle with a b, draw b d parallel to **a** c. With any distance as a unit, lay off on the lines from a and b as many equal spaces as the number of parts required. Join 4 b, 3 e, 2 f, 1 g and a h.

Fig. 13. To bisect any angle as a b c. With b as a center and any radius, draw a c, then with a and c as centers and any radius greater than one-half of **a** c, draw arcs intersecting in d. Draw b d.

Fig. 14. To construct an angle equal to a given angle e b c. Dray any line as d f. With b as a center and any radius, cut the sides of the given angle in c and e. With d as a center and the same radius, draw arc f g. With c e as a radius and f as a center cut arc f g in g. Join d g.

Fig. 15. To describe an angle of 30° and 60°. From a, with any radius draw the arc c d, and from c with the same radius cut it in d, let fall a perpendicular d b; then c a d equals 60°, and a d b equals 30°.

Fig. 16. To divide a circle into twelve equal parts with the T square, and 30° x 60° triangle. Draw a b with the T square. Next draw e e with the short side of the triangle on the T square, and the next longest side directed to the center of the circle. Draw c c and g g with either of the longest sides of the triangle on the T square, and the other directed to the center of the circle. Draw d d and f f with the shortest side of the triangle on the T square, and the longest side directed to the center of the circle.

Fig. 17. To draw this square draw the circle first, then with the T square and triangle draw horizontal and vertical lines tangent to the circle.

Fig. 18. To draw a hexagon with the T square and triangle. Draw the circle first, then with the 30° x 60° triangle and T square, draw lines tangent to the circle.

Fig. 19. To draw an octagon with the T square and triangle. Draw the circle first, then with the 45° triangle and T square, draw lines tangent to the circle.

Fig. 20. To draw a pentagon upon a line, as a b. Draw b c perpendicular to a b, and equal to one-half of it ; produce a c until c d is equal to b c. From a and b, with radius b d draw arcs cutting each other in e ; then from e with radius e b, draw circle a f b. Line a b is equal to one side of the pentagon.

Fig. 21. To draw an approximate ellipse. Let a b be the major axis and c d the minor axis of an ellipse. With aʰ as a center and radius aʰ d, draw arc d e. Join d b. Make d f equal to b e. Bisect b f by a perpendicular, intersecting d c in h. g b will be the radius for the ends of the ellipse, and h d the radius for the sides. Make aʰ c′ equal to aʰ g, and aʰ cʰ equal to aʰ h.

Plate 2.

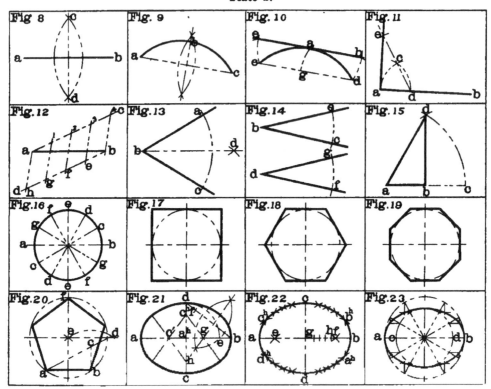

Fig. 22. To draw an ellipse. Let a b be the major axis and d c the minor axis. With d as a center and radius g a, draw arcs cutting a b in e and f which are the foci. Between g and f take any point as h, and with f and e as centers and radius h b, draw arcs as at aʰ bʰ dʰ cʰ, then with the same centers and h a as a radius, draw arcs intersecting those first drawn. Take any other points between g and f and repeat the operation as is shown. Through the intersection of these arcs draw the curve of the ellipse.

Fig. 23. To draw an ellipse from two concentric circles. Draw two circles, as a b, c d, diameters of which are respectively lengths of major and minor axis. Divide the circle a b into about twelve equal parts, and draw radial lines. The intersection of the horizontal and vertical lines drawn from the radial lines will give points in the curve of the ellipse.

Plate 8.

Fig. 24. To make a mechanical drawing of a block 4″ high by 3″ wide and 1¾″ thick.

NOTE.—When an object revolves parallel with a plane, its projections on that plane are in their true length, but when it makes an angle with the plane, its projections on that plane will not be in their true length. Therefore the first view of the object must be on the plane with which it is parallel, but as all the views in Fig. 24 are parallel with all the planes, we can draw any of them first. In a case of this kind, however, it would be well to draw the top or plan first.

Then let g^h g^h and f^v f^v be the axes about which the planes of projection revolve. Draw the plan to the dimensions given. Project a^h to a^v in the front elevation and produce it to b^v, making a^v b^v 4″ long and project d^h to d^v produced to c^v. Connect a^v d^v, c^v b^v, thus completing the front elevation. Now project a^h to f, and e^h to d, in f^v f^v. With center g and radius g f, draw the arc f c ; now with the same center and radius g d, draw arc d a. Then c projected to the side elevation and intersected by the projection of the top of the block a^v d^v in the front elevation, will locate a''' in the side elevation, and a''' produced to intersect the projection of a will give e'''. The projection of the bottom of the block intersected by the projection from c and a, will give b'' g''. Connect the points and complete the drawing.

Fig. 25. This is a drawing of the same block inclined at an angle of 30° with the side vertical plane. Here it will be oblique to the horizontal and side vertical planes, therefore we cannot draw either of these views first. But as it revolves through this angle it remains parallel with the front vertical plane, therefore it is on this plane we must draw the first view. Having found which plane to draw on first, proceed to draw the block in full as shown in the front elevation. Then lay off the thickness in the plan and side views to the dimensions given, and from the corners in the front view project to the plan and side views, as a^v to a^h, and b^h and a^v to a'' and b''. Follow the instructions of Fig. 24 and complete the drawing.

Figs. 26 and 27 represent the same block in different positions and are drawn by the principles illustrated in Figs. 24 and 25.

Plate 3.

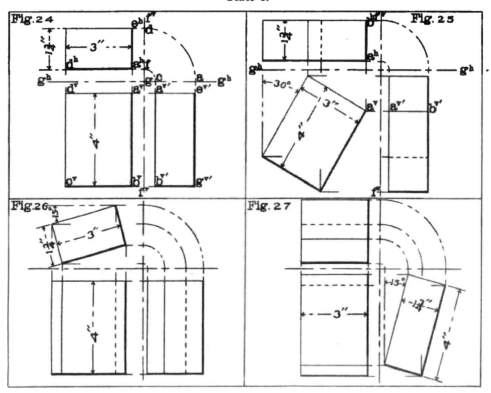

Plate 4.

Figs. 28 and 29 are drawings of a block to be drawn as shown from the instructions on Figs. 24 and 25, plate 3.

Fig. 30. This is the same block revolved so as to make an angle of 15° with the side vertical plane. But a' b' in this revolution will remain the same distance from the front vertical plane, therefore it follows from what has been said respecting Fig. 25 that the front elevation must be drawn first. Make a' b', Fig. 30, equal to a' b', Fig. 29, at an angle as shown. Then make a' f', Fig. 30, perpendicular to a' b', Fig. 30, and equal to a' f', Fig. 29. The distance a' g', etc., is equal to a' g', etc., Fig. 29. From these points draw lines parallel to a' b', also from b' parallel to a' f'. To draw the plan: From f', c', etc., project fine lines which will pass through fʰ, cʰ, gʰ, aʰ. Now take the distances from the axis gʰ gʰ, Fig. 29, to cʰ, fʰ, aʰ, gʰ and lay off these distances from the axis gʰ gʰ, Fig. 30, on the lines already projected. They will locate the corresponding letters in Fig. 30, and the points being connected will give the top of the block. The bottom is found in the same way. The side elevation can be projected from the views already drawn if cʰ be projected to the axis fʰ fʰ, and from the intersection of fʰ fʰ with gʰ gʰ as a center, we revolve cʰ to gʰ gʰ and project cʰ down until it intersects c', projected from the front elevation, and thus locate c'' in the side elevation. All other points are located in the same way.

Fig. 31. In this figure the block makes an angle of 15° with the front vertical plane. From what has already been said we see that the side view must be drawn first. Draw c'' e'' at an angle of 15° and equal to c'' e'', Fig. 30. Then draw a perpendicular c d and also a perpendicular a b from c'' e'', Fig. 30, about midway between c'' e''. Make the distance from c'' e'' to a'' b'', etc., measured on c d equal the corresponding distances in Fig. 30. The distances from c d to c'' a'', etc., are the same as from a b to c'' a'', etc, Fig. 30. Project f' c'', etc., to the front view and make the distance from f' f' to f' c', etc., in the front view, Fig. 31, the same as from f' f' to f' c', etc., in the front view, Fig. 30. The bottom is found in the same way. The top view can be projected from the front and side views as the side view was projected in Fig. 30.

Plate 4.

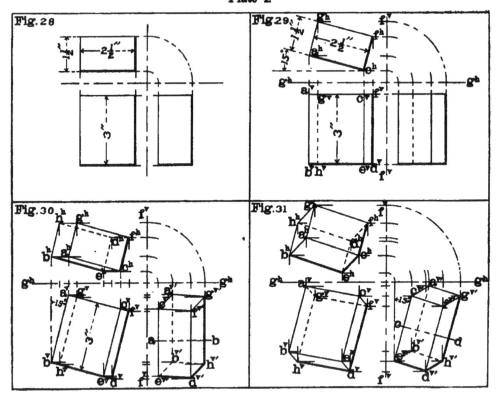

Fig. 28

Fig. 29

Fig. 30

Fig. 31

Plate 5.

All big things are made up of a number of little things assembled. This is true regardless of size. Therefore, the big things cannot be done unless we are able to do the little things. How important it is then, that the little things should be remembered, to think differently is deceiving one's own self, which is the worst deception any person can be guilty of. Be honest with yourself, then with a purpose in view followed diligently, there is no reason why any person should not succeed. The big things a man can do, is governed by the number of little things he has to assemble.

Fig. 32. This is a drawing and development of a vertical cylinder, 2½ inches diameter, and cut by a cutting plane which intersects the axis 2 inches above the base. To draw this cylinder: Draw the line $a^h b^h$, which will be the trace of a central vertical plane parallel to the front vertical plane of projection. Also, draw the line $f^v f^v$, which will be the trace of a central vertical plane perpendicular to the front vertical plane of projection. The intersection of these planes will be the axis of the cylinder. From the intersection of these planes as a center, and with the compass set to a radius of 1¼ inches, draw the circle as shown. Then draw the base line $c^v c^v$, and vertical projecting lines tangent to the circle cutting the base line in the points c^v and c^v. Lay off from the base on $f^v f^v$ 2 inches, and through this point draw the line $d^v d^v$, at a angle of 45° to the axis of the cylinder, which will be the trace of the cutting plane. If the top of the cylinder be projected upon a plane, parallel to $d^v d^v$, the true size of the section of the cylinder will be obtained. To do this it will be necessary to pass a number of auxiliary planes. These planes should be vertical, and parallel to the front vertical plane of projection. To do this, divide the circle in the plan, into, say 12 equal parts, then, through these points draw traces as shown, which will be the traces of the auxiliary planes. Also, from these same points and parallel to $f^v f^v$, draw projecting lines to the front elevation as shown. At any convenient distance, and parallel to $d^v d^v$, draw the line $c^h d^h$, which will be a trace of the central vertical plane $a^h b^h$. Now draw the vertical line $e^v e^v$, which will be a trace of the same central vertical plane. Next draw traces the same distance from $c^h d^h$ and $e^v e^v$, as the traces in the plan are from $a^h b^h$. Then projections from the points in the front elevation, where the traces on the surface of the cylinder, intersect the trace of the cutting plane to the corresponding traces in the auxiliary view, and side elevation, will give points through which to draw the curve. The base in the auxiliary view is drawn in the same manner. See the indications.

To Draw the Development: Draw the line e g, the length of which is equal to the diameter of the cylinder multiplied by 3.1416. As the circle is divided into 12 equal parts, this line must be divided into the same number of equal parts. From each one of the points thus obtained erect perpendiculars as shown, and make their height equal to the corresponding line in the front elevation. Through the points thus found draw the curve, and thereby complete the development.

Auxiliary planes may be taken in any position, yet for simplicity and clearness, they should be in such a position as to cut straight lines, or a circle from the cylinder if possible. Any plane which is parallel to the axis of a cylinder will cut the surface in straight lines, and any plane which is perpendicular to the axis will cut it in a circle. Any plane which passes through the apex of a cone will cut the surface in straight lines, any plane which is perpendicular to the axis of a cone, will cut the surface in a circle, and any plane which is oblique to the axis and cuts opposite sides of the cone will cut the surface in an ellipse, which should be avoided if possible.

Plate 5.

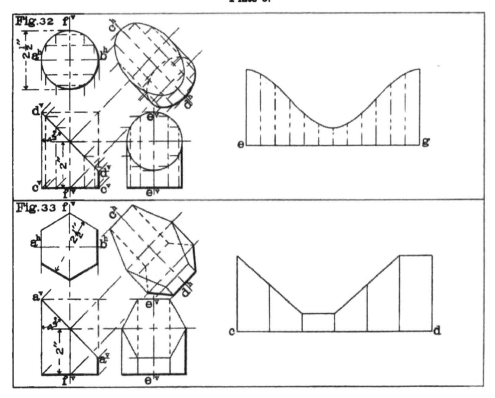

Fig. 33. This is a drawing and development of a vertical hexagonal prism. By observing the letters in the plate, and the explanation of Fig. 32, there should be no difficulty experienced in making this drawing. Therefore, after a word about the development it will be left to the pupil. Take the length of one side of the hexagon from the plan, and lay it off six times on the line c d, which will give the length of the development. The pupil should bear in mind that the distance any line or point is to the right of the central vertical plane in the side elevation, is the same as the distance the same line or point is in the rear of the central vertical plane in the plan; and all lines or points to the left of the central vertical plane in the side elevation are the same distance, as the same lines or points are in front of the central vertical plane in the plan. This is a general statement, and should be remembered.

Plate 6.

Fig. 34. This is a drawing of a vertical cone to the dimensions given, drawn to locate the points c and b. Draw the plan and front view first. Then drew d' d parallel to the side of the cone, which is a trace of the central vertical plane f^h g^h. Draw the line b' a' perpendicular to d' d to intersect the plane of the base of the cone at a', and project a' to the plan as at a^h. Draw a^h c^h tangent to the base of the cone and project c^h to c'. Draw the ellipse of the base in the oblique view as instructed in Fig. 32, plate 5. Project c' to c and b, and b' to d'. Draw c d' and b d'

Fig. 35. This is a drawing of a hexagonal prism to the dimensions given. From what has already been said, the pupil should have no difficulty with this ·lrawing, and should be able to do it without further instructions.

Fig. 36. This is a drawing of a vertical pyramid with a pentagonal base, cut by a cutting plane as shown. Draw the pentagon as instructed in Fig. 20, plate 2. Then from each corner in the base draw lines to the center, which are the corners of the pyramid. Now draw the front and side elevations of the pyramid, and in the front elevation draw the trace of the cutting plane as shown. If the points where the corners of the pyramid intersect this trace be projected to the corresponding lines in the plan and side elevation, all of the points will be located except f^h, which may be located as indicated in the figure.

Fig. 37. This is a drawing of a vertical hexagonal pyramid, cut by a cutting plane parallel to the front vertical plane. No difficulty should be experienced in working it out as the work is similar to Fig. 36.

Plate 6.

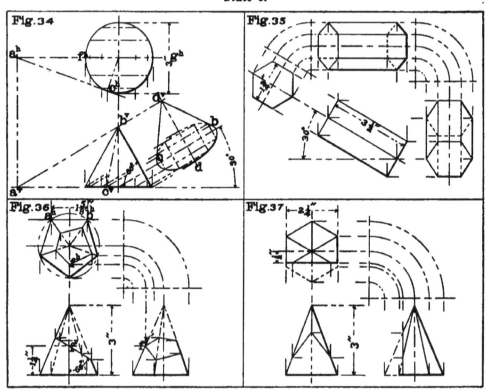

Fig.34   Fig.35   Fig.36   Fig.37

Plate 7.

Fig. 38. This is a drawing and development of a vertical pyramid with a hexagonal base, cut by a cutting plane as shown. Draw the plan, front and side elevations, and the trace of the cutting plane in the front elevation, and proceed as instructed in Fig. 36, plate 6. The true form of the section made by the cutting plane passing through the pyramid is found as follows: At any convenient distance from the cutting plane, and parallel to it, draw the line a b, which is a trace of the central vertical plane $a^h b^h$. From the points in the front elevation where the corners of the pyramid intersect the trace of the cutting plane draw projecting lines as indicated. All the points in this auxiliary view are the same distance from a b, as the corresponding points are from $a^h b^h$, as c′ d′ is equal to $c^h d^h$. All other points are located in the same manner.

To DRAW THE DEVELOPMENT: From f as a center and e′ g′ as a radius draw the arc c a e. With $g^h d^h$ as a chord, step three times each side of a. Join these points by straight lines; and from the same points draw straight lines to f. From the points in the front elevation where the corners of the pyramid intersect the trace of the cutting plane, project to e′ g′ as indicated in the Fig. Take the length e′ f′ and lay it off from f on the lines f e and f c, and thus locate b and g. Make f h and f h′ equal to e′ b′, and locate the remaining points in the same manner.

Fig. 39. This is a drawing and development of a vertical cone cut by a cutting plane as shown. Draw the plan, the front and the side elevations, and in the front elevation draw the trace of the cutting plane as shown. Also draw the auxiliary view on a plane parallel to the cutting plane. We have now to pass a number of auxiliary planes in order to determine points on the line of intersection of the cutting plane with the surface of the cone. This may be done as follows: Divide the circle of the base in the plan into twelve equal parts, and lines drawn from these points to the center will be traces of vertical planes which pass through the apex of the cone. From where these traces intersect the circle of the base in the plan, draw projecting lines to the base in the front elevation, and lines drawn from these points to the apex will be traces of the same vertical planes; also make projections to the side elevation and auxiliary view as indicated, draw the traces as shown and proceed as in the case of the pyramid, Fig. 38.

To DRAW THE DEVELOPMENT: .With the length of the side of the cone as a radius, draw an arc, also a center line as shown in the development. The length of this arc is equal to the circumference of the base of the cone and may be measured by stepping off on this arc the divisions in the plan, that is the arc v v is equal to the arc h h, and so on. From these points draw lines to the apex. Then from where the traces in the front elevation intersect the trace of the cutting plane project to the outside line of the cone and proceed as in the case of the development of the pyramid, Fig. 38.

Plate 7.

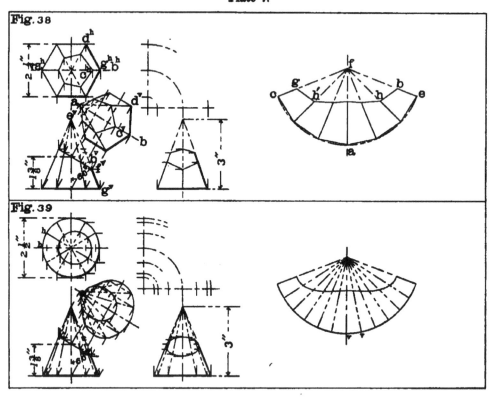

Fig. 38

Fig. 39

Plate 8.

Fig. 40. This is a drawing and development of a vertical cone, of the dimensions given, cut by a plane parallel to the base. From what has already been said the pupil should be able to make this drawing without further instruction. The development is similar to the development in Fig. 39, plate 7.

Fig. 41. This is a drawing and development of a vertical cone of the dimensions given, cut by a vertical plane ½ inch in front of the axis. The section in the front elevation made by this plane will be bounded by a curve, and in order to find this curve we must pass auxiliary planes. Draw the plan, front and side elevations in full, and draw parallel to the axis in the plan and side elevation and ½ inch from it, $c^h e^h$ and $c'' a''$. $c^h e^h$ is a horizontal trace of the cutting plane, and $c'' a''$ is a vertical trace of the same plane. From the point where the trace $c'' a''$ intersects the side of the cone project to a^v and thus locate the highest point in the curve. We are now ready to pass the auxiliary planes, which for accuracy in the construction of the curve should be horizontal as shown by the traces in the front elevation. Locate any number of points as 1, 2, 3, etc., and through them pass the auxiliary planes. From where these traces intersect the side of the cone in the front elevation draw projecting lines to the trace of the central vertical plane in the plan as indicated. Through the points thus located describe circles which are traces of the same horizontal planes. From the points where these circular traces intersect the trace of the cutting plane project to the corresponding traces in the front elevation as indicated. Through these points draw the curve, which is a hyperbola, and is the true shape of the section of the cone, made by the intersection of the surface of the cone with the trace of the vertical cutting plane. A hyperbola is a curve formed by a section of a cone, when the cutting plane makes a greater angle with the base than the side of the cone makes. If the cutting plane is parallel to one of the sides of a cone, the curve formed by the intersection of the surface of the cone with the trace of the cutting plane, will be a parabola.

To Draw the Development: The best way to do this is to pass a series of vertical auxiliary planes. Locate points in the base as h^h, g^h, etc., and project them to the front and side elevations, and draw the traces as shown. Then from where these traces intersect the trace of the vertical cutting plane in the side elevation project to the side of the cone as indicated. With the indication in connection with the explanation of Fig. 39, plate 7, the development should be completed without difficulty.

Fig. 42. This is a drawing and development of a vertical cone of the dimensions given, cut by a cutting plane, which is parallel to one side of the cone, and intersects the base, one inch from the central vertical plane. Draw the plan, front and side elevations in full. In the front elevation draw the trace of the cutting plane as shown, and pass a series of auxiliary planes as instructed in Fig. 41. From the points in the front elevation where the traces of the auxiliary planes intersect the trace of the cutting plane project to the corresponding circular traces

Plate 8.

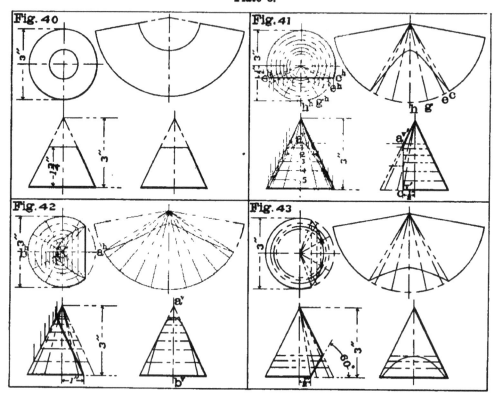

in the plan, and thus locate the points through which to draw the curve. In the side elevation, the distance from the central vertical plane a′ b′ to the points in the traces of the auxiliary planes through which the curve must pass, are equal to the distances which the corresponding points in the circular traces of the corresponding planes are from the same central vertical plane aʰ bʰ in the plan. Proceed with the development as in Fig. 41.

Fig. 43 is similar, and should be drawn without difficulty.

Plate 9.

Fig. 44. This is a drawing of a vertical cone of the dimensions given, cut by a cutting plane as shown in the front elevation. Draw the plan, front and side elevations in full. Now draw the trace of the cutting plane, and at any convenient distance and parallel to it draw the trace a b. If any difficulty should be experienced refer to Figs. 41 and 42, plate 8. The ellipse in the auxiliary view is the true shape, made by the intersection of the surface of the cone with the trace of the cutting plane, because it is on a plane which is parallel to the cutting plane.

Fig. 45. This is a drawing of a vertical cone, intersected by a horizontal cylinder whose axis intersects the axis of the cone 1⅛ inches above its base. Draw the plan, front and side elevations in full, excepting the curve of intersection which is to be determined. The curve of intersection of any two solids may be determined by passing a series of auxiliary planes through the two solids. As already explained any plane which is parallel to the axis of a cylinder will cut it in straight lines ; and any plane which passes through the apex of a cone will cut it in straight lines. Draw lines as shown in the side elevation, which will be the traces of planes passing through the apex of the cone and parallel to the axis of the cylinder. Be sure to draw a″ b and a″ a‴ tangent to the cylinder. When the axes of the solids intersect—as they do in this case—the spaces a‴ i, etc., should be equal to b r, etc. From where the circle intersects these traces, draw horizontal lines as shown on the surface of the cylinder in the front elevation. Now project b to the circle of the base in the plan and thus locate bʰ and cʰ. Draw lines from bʰ and cʰ to a. Project bʰ and cʰ to the base in the front elevation and thus locate bᵛ and cᵛ, also draw lines from bᵛ and cᵛ to aᵛ. The lines aᵛ bᵛ, aᵛ cᵛ, a bʰ and a cʰ are the traces of a plane which passes through the apex of the cone, and tangent to the cylinder. The point where the trace aᵛ bᵛ on the surface of the cone intersects the trace made on the surface of the cylinder by the same plane, will be one point in the curve, as at f. Then f projected to the corresponding trace in the plan, will locate the point in the plan, as at fʰ. In like manner locate the remaining points, and through them draw the curve of intersection.

Fig. 46. This is a drawing of a vertical cone, intersected by a horizontal cylinder, the axis of which is ¼ inch in front of the axis of the cone, and 1¼ inches above the base of the latter. Further explanation is unnecessary, as the work is similar to Fig. 45.

Fig. 47. This is a drawing of a vertical pyramid with a square base intersected by a horizontal cylinder as shown. The curve of intersection of these two solids may be determined by passing a series of vertical auxiliary planes as shown in the side elevation. Draw the vertical trace k j tangent to the cylinder. The spaces j l, l i and i r may be equal or unequal, it is better, however, to make them unequal as shown. If the divisions are equal, some of the divisions on the circle will be exceedingly long, and others exceedingly short, which will make some of the points in the curve of intersection very far apart, and others very close. This should be avoided if possible.

Plate 9.

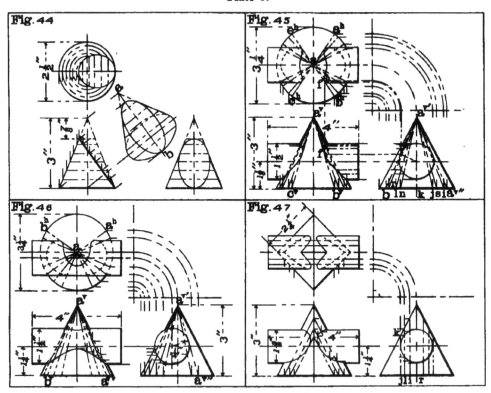

Plate 10.

Fig. 48. This is a drawing and development of a vertical cylinder intersected by two horizontal cylinders, as shown. After all the views have been drawn in full, divide the circle at the right (which is the end view of the horizontal cylinder) into, say twelve equal parts, draw lines as shown and make the projections to the plan and front elevation as indicated in the plate. These lines are traces of vertical planes parallel with the axis of the cylinder, and will cut the surface of the cylinder in straight lines. The traces of these vertical planes having already been drawn in the plan and front elevation of the horizontal cylinder the next thing to be done is to project the points where these traces intersect the vertical cylinder to the traces of the same vertical planes in the front elevation, which will give the points through which the curve of intersection must be drawn. After the above explanation there should be no difficulty with the one on the left.

To draw the developments of these cylinders one has simply to unroll their surfaces until they are in one plane as shown in the plate. Suppose the vertical cylinder begins to unroll at c^h, then c^h will be at c^r in the development, and h^h at h^r, and g^h at g^r, and f^h at f^r, and d^h at d^r, and b^h at b^r, and so on all the way round the cylinder to c^h where the start was made. Draw traces from each of these points which will be in the same position as they were before the surface was unrolled. The points of intersection upon these traces through which the development of the intersection is drawn, are the same distance above the line c^r d as the corresponding points are above the base of the vertical cylinder in the front elevation. The horizontal cylinders will be left for the pupil without further explanation.

Fig. 49. This is a drawing and developments of a vertical cylinder intersected on the right by a cylinder whose axis makes an angle of $45°$ with the axis of the vertical cylinder; and on the left by a horizontal cylinder which is tangent to the vertical cylinder. In a case like the one on the right where the axes of the cylinders are oblique to each other, the auxiliary planes should be parallel to both axes. They will cut both surfaces in straight lines.

With the lines and letters which are shown in the plate, the pupil has all the information necessary to finish the drawing.

Plate 10.

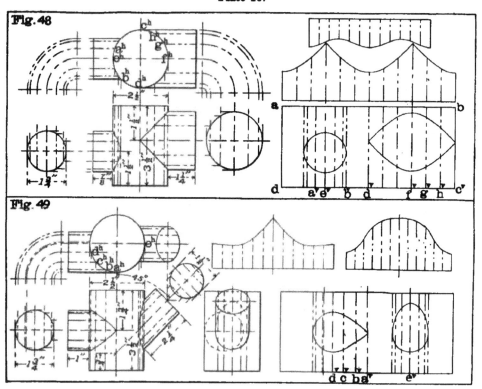

Fig. 48

Fig. 49

Plate 11.

Fig. 50. This a drawing and development of a horizontal cylinder intersected by two vertical cylinders as shown.

With some study of this plate in connection with the explanation of plate 10, there should be no difficulty experienced with this drawing and the developments.

Plate 11.

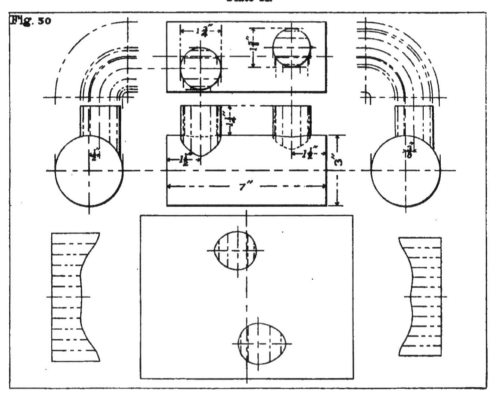

Plate 12.

Fig. 51. This is a drawing and development of a vertical cylinder cut by a cutting plane which makes an angle of 60° with the central vertical plane. This plane intersects the top of the cylinder in the axis, and is at such an angle as to intersect the base 1 inch from the axis. $a^h d^h$, is the trace of this plane at the top, and $c^h f^h$, is the trace at the base. Divide the distance between the traces in the plan into, say two equal parts, and draw the trace $b^h e^h$. Divide the height in the front elevation into the same number of equal parts and draw the trace $b^v e^v$. Make projections from the plan to the front and side elevation as indicated by the letters. This vertical cylinder is also intersected on the left by a horizontal cylinder, the axis of which is ¼ inch in front of the axis of the vertical cylinder. This is drawn in the same manner as instructed in plate 10.

To draw the development. If the cylinder in the plan be divided into twelve equal parts, one of these parts taken and laid off twelve times on a straight line will give the length of the development. By referring to the letters, there should be no difficulty in completing the development so far as the right hand side is concerned. Remember that the width of the spaces in the opening for the horizontal cylinder on the left is equal to the length of the arcs in the plan, as v v is equal to the arc h h in the plan and the remaining spaces in like manner.

Fig. 52. This is a drawing and development of an inclined cylinder, the axis of which is at an angle of 60° with the horizontal plane, the base and top being parallel with the horizontal plane.

This cylinder is also intersected on the left by a horizontal cylinder as shown. To draw the development of this inclined cylinder. Draw the development as previously instructed except the opening for the horizontal cylinder. The development having been drawn it will be seen that the top and base have developed into curves of which v v, g^v v v, is the one for the top. Then it will be seen that the length of the arcs in the plan between the sides of the horizontal cylinder, one of which is h h, must be laid off on this curve to obtain the points through which to draw the traces from which to determine the opening for the horizontal cylinder. v v, and v v, are each equal to the arc h h, continue with the others in like manner.

The pupil should have enough ingenuity to finish the drawing.

Plate 12.

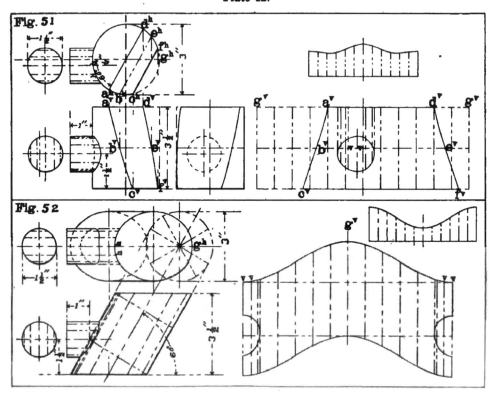

Plate 13.

Fig. 53. This is a drawing and development of a vertical hexagonal pyramid intersected by a horizontal cylinder. Draw all three views in full first. Divide each side of the base in the plan into four equal parts. From these points draw lines to the apex, these lines will be the traces of planes passing through the apex of the pyramid and parallel to the axis of the cylinder. Project these same points to the base in the front and side elevations, and draw lines from these points in the base to the apex. These lines will be traces of the same planes, and their intersection with the cylinder in the side elevation will be points to project to the corresponding traces in the front elevation and plan.

To Draw the Development: With b″ h″ as a radius, and b‴ as a center draw an arc. With one side of the base in the plan as a chord step off six times on the arc. Connect each one of these points with straight lines, and also, draw lines from the same points to the apex. These lines are equal in length to b″ h″, and are the corners of the pyramid. If the points where the lines which represent the corners of the pyramid intersect the cylinder be projected to b″ h″, the distance from b″ to the points found by projection will be the distance to lay off on the corresponding lines in the development from b‴. On account of the curve in the development it will be necessary to draw lines in the development midway between those already drawn, which will be the same as the traces in the plan midway between the corners. b″ h″ is the true length of the corners, because it is parallel to the plane on which it is projected, therefore b′ e′ is the true length of b^h e^h and all other lines midway between the corners. If the points where the curve of intersection intersects these traces in the front elevation be projected to b′ e′, the distance from b′ to the points found by projection will be the distance to lay off on the corresponding line in the development from b‴.

Plate 13.

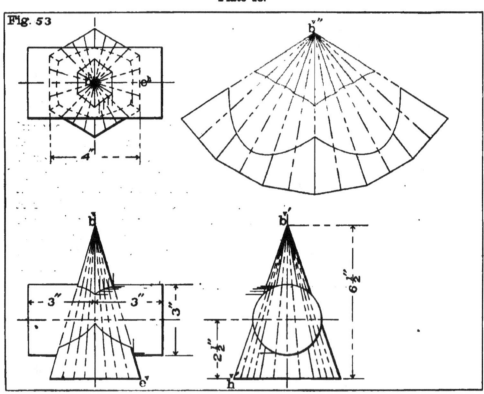

Fig. 53

Plate 14.

Fig. 54. This is a drawing and development of a vertical hexagonal pyramid intersected by a horizontal cylinder. The axis of the cylinder is parallel to both planes of projection, and $\frac{1}{4}$ inch in front of the axis of the pyramid. Draw all three views in full, and proceed as instructed in Fig. 53, plate 13, except the trace a″ b″, which is tangent to the cylinder in the side elevation. a^h is the same distance from the central vertical plane as a″ is from f″. The point c″ can be located by drawing a line through the center of the cylinder and perpendicular to a″ b″. Then if it is projected to the traces of the same plane in the front elevation and plan c′ and c^h will be located. $g^h c^h$ is the distance that c‴ is from b‴, and is found by making $g^h b^h$ equal to c′ f′ and perpendicular to $b^h a^h$. Further instruction is unnecessary as the work is similar to Fig. 53, plate 13.

Plate 14.

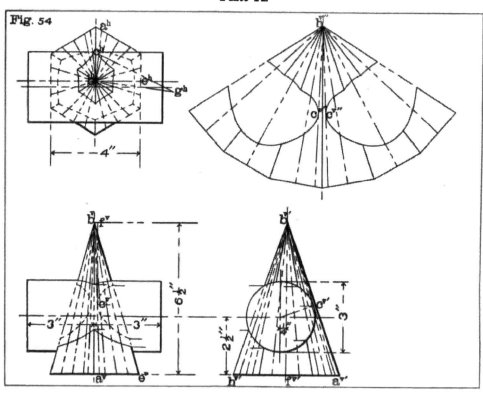

Fig. 54

Plate 15.

Fig. 55. This is a drawing of a vertical pyramid with a triangular base, and the front side making an angle of 15° with the front vertical plane, intersected by a triangular prism with its axis parallel with both planes of projection, the front side making an angle of 15° with the front vertical plane and drawn to the dimensions given. If we use the line f' g', which is the top corner of the prism, as the trace of a cutting plane, it will give a triangular section in the plan as a⁰ b⁰ c⁰. Where the traces of this section intersect the line fʰ gʰ (which is the same corner of the prism) will be points of intersection of the two solids, because fʰ gʰ and aʰ bʰ cʰ are in the same plane, and these points dʰ eʰ projected back to f' g', will give the points d' e' in the front elevation. All other points are found in the same way, except where the left corner of the pyramid is cut. Use the line forming the corner of the pyramid as the trace of a cutting plane, and where it intersects the lines of the prism project to the corresponding lines in the plan, which will give a section of the prism in the same plane as the corner of the pyramid is. Where the traces of this section intersect the corner of the pyramid will be the required points of intersection, and if projected back to the front elevation, will give the points there. The pupil should study these principles, as he will have many cases of their application.

Plate 15.

Fig. 55

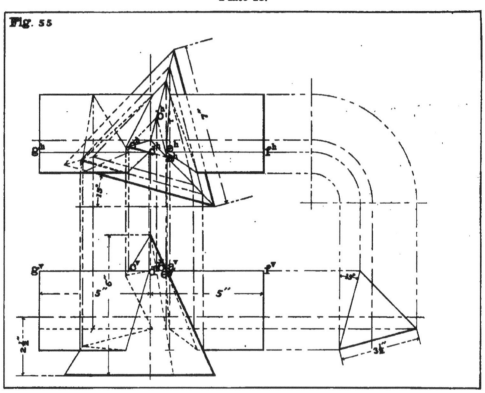

Plate 16.

Fig. 56. This is a drawing of a vertical pyramid with triangular base, making an angle of 15° with the side vertical plane, intersected by a triangular prism, the axis of which is parallel with the vertical plane, ½ inch in the rear of the axis of the pyramid and making an angle of 30° with the horizontal plane. The bottom side makes an angle of 15° with the horiozontal plane. The intersection of these two solids can be found in the same way as Fig. 55, plate 15, but there are other ways, and it would be well if the pupil would use other lines as traces of cutting planes. Suppose we use the line $a^h\ b^h$ as the trace of a cutting plane. Where that trace intersects the base of the pyramid in the plan it should be projected to the base in the front elevation, and where the same trace intersects the front corner in the plan it should be projected to the corresponding line in the front elevation. Draw traces from that point to the points already found in the base, and where these traces intersect $a^v\ b^v$ will be the required points of intersection, because they are in the same plane. If the pupil will have patience to find one point at a time in making these drawings, any of them should be handled without difficulty.

Plate 16.

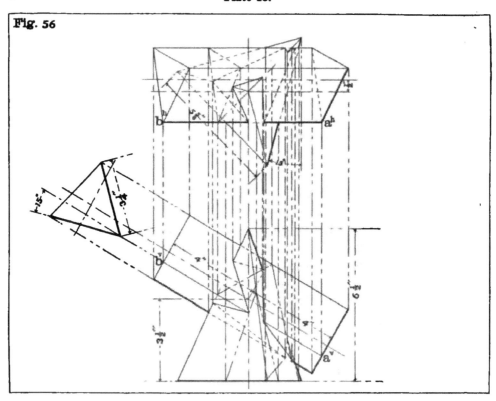

Fig. 56

Plate 17.

Fig. 57. This is a drawing of axes or center lines oblique to both planes of projection, about which any solid may be drawn very readily. Draw $b^v b^v$, which will be the trace of a horizontal plane; then f f perpendicular to $b^v b^v$ and $a^v c^v$ at the desired angle ($45°$) with the horizontal plane, making it of any convenient length longer than the length of the object to be drawn. Draw also $c^v c^h$ any convenient length. Now draw $c^h a$, making the desired angle with the front vertical plane. From a^h to h^v draw a line perpendicular to $c^h a$ and $g^v e^v$ parallel to $c^h a$, and any convenient distance from $c^h a$. Then $c^h e^v$ must be parallel to $a^h h^v$. Make $g^v h^v$ equal to the vertical distance that c^v is from $b^v b^v$. Draw $d^v d^v$ through h^v and parallel to $g^v e^v$, which will be a trace of the horizontal plane $b^v b^v$. Now draw a line from h^v to e^v, which will be the true length of the axis $a^v c^v$, and will also be a parallel view of the axis. Here we must draw the object first in its true size. The line $c^v f^v$ may, for convenience in drawing, be equal to $c^v c^h$. If $c^v c^h$ be produced to intersect a horizontal from a^h as at b, then the distance c^v b, laid off on $c^v f^v$ produced as at c, and projected to $b^v b^v$, will give f^v, and $f^v f^v$ is a side view of the axis.

Fig. 58. This is a drawing of a solid inclined to both planes of projection as shown. The axis must be drawn in full first, as instructed in Fig. 57. If it is true that the distance $g^v h^v$ is equal to the vertical distance from c^v to $b^v b^v$, it is also true that the vertical distance from c^v to any point in the front or side views is equal to the distance from $g^v e^v$ to the corresponding point in the auxiliary view, taken perpendicular to $g^v e^v$. Draw the auxiliary first as shown. The top view can be projected from the auxiliary view, and the thickness taken from the end view. The front view can be projected from the top, and the vertical distances of all the points found as already explained. The side view is not shown, but must be drawn by the pupil. It can be done by projecting all the corners from top and front views.

Fig. 59. This is a drawing of a triangular prism of the dimensions shown, and can be drawn from instructions already given.

Fig. 60. This is a drawing of a cube of the dimensions given, and if the others on the plate are understood there will be no difficulty in drawing it. A thorough knowledge of these principles is something that no draughtsman can afford to be without; therefore it is hoped that the pupil will give this plate undivided attention and study.

Plate 17.

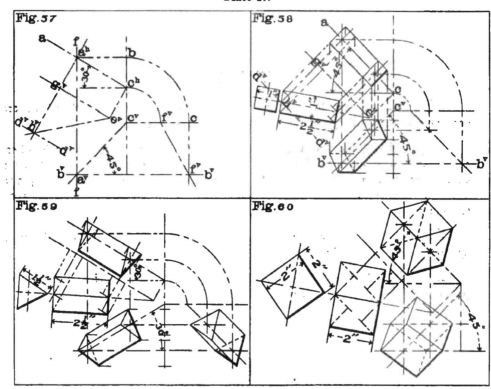

Fig. 57

Fig. 58

Fig. 59

Fig. 60

Plate 18.

Fig. 61. When the axes of cones, cylinders, pyramids, and prisms are parallel, choose auxiliary planes perpendicular to the axes.

Fig. 62. When the axes of cone and cylinder are oblique to each other, choose auxiliary planes passing through the apex of the cone and parallel to the axis of the cylinder. When the axes of two cones are perpendicular or oblique to each other, choose auxiliary planes passing through a line which contains the apex of each cone.

Fig. 63. This drawing differs from Fig. 54, plate 17, only in being a cylinder, and will give the pupil an opportunity to unfold his ingenuity.

Fig. 64. This drawing differs from Fig. 54, only in being a hexagonal prism, and should be drawn without any difficulty whatever.

Plate 18.

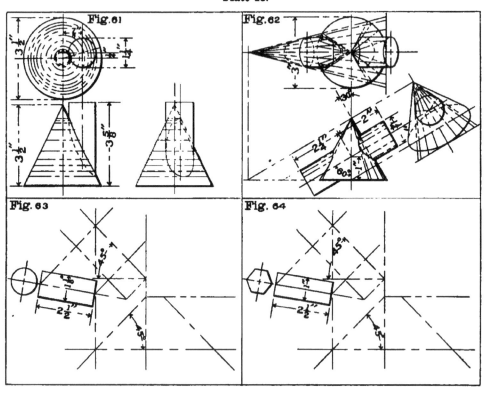

Fig. 61

Fig. 62

Fig. 63

Fig. 64

Plate 19.

Fig. 65. This is a drawing and development of a hexagonal pyramid, the base of which is parallel with the horizontal plane. It is intersected by a square prism, the axis of which is parallel with the front vertical plane of projection, and is $\frac{7}{8}$ of an inch in the rear of the axis of the pyramid, and makes an angle of 30° with the horizontal plane.

After the plan and front elevation have been drawn in full, proceed to determine the intersections of the two solids. This may be done in the following manner: Produce the right and left corners of the pyramid in the plan until they intersect the ends of the prism as shown at a^h, b^h, c^h, d^h, then project from these intersections to the prism in the front elevation as at a^v, b^v, c^v, d^v. A trace from a^v, to c^v, will give the point of intersection in the right hand corner of the pyramid as seen at g^v, and a trace from b^v, to d^v, will give the point e^v, in the right hand corner of the pyramid, and f^v in the left hand corner of the pyramid. These points projected back to the same corners in the plan will give the points g^h, e^h, and f^h. If the two rear corners of the pyramid be produced until they intersect the rear corner of the prism a^{hh} b^{hh}, in the points c^{hh}, d^{hh}, these intersections should be projected to the corner a^{vv} b^{vv}, in the front elevation. The points where the same corners of the pyramid intersects the corners e^{hh} g^{hh}, and f^{hh} h^{hh}, of the prism should be projected to the corresponding corners in the front elevation. Also project the intersection of the right hand front corner of the pyramid with the front corner of the prism, to the corresponding corner in the front elevation. All of these points connected as shown by the traces in the front elevation, will give the points of intersection of the corners of the pyramid with the prism, and these points projected back to the corresponding corners in the plan will give the points there.

From the explanation already given, in connection with the traces for the remaining points it would seem that there should be no difficulty in completing the intersection of these two solids.

To draw the development. With the length of the right hand corner of the pyramid in the front elevation as a radius draw an arc of a circle, then with the length of one side of the base taken from the plan, lay it off six times on the arc of a circle already drawn; connect these points with straight lines, also from the same points draw lines to the apex. Project the intersections of each corner of the pyramid in the front elevation to the right hand corner of the pyramid, and the distance from these projections to the apex will be the distance to lay off on the corresponding corners in the development. This having been done, the next thing in order is to locate the points where the corners of the prism intersect the pyramid. This may be done as follows: From the apex in the plan draw traces through the points where the corners of the prism intersect the pyramid until they intersect the base as shown at a, b, c, d, e. The distance that each one of these points a, b, c, d, e, is from the adjoining corner of the pyramid should be laid off in the development, and the traces drawn as shown. The points of intersection of the corners of the prism with the pyramid, will fall on these auxiliary traces, and may be located in the following manner. The point where the top corner of the prism intersects the pyramid on the left should be projected to either outside corner of the pyramid in the front elevation; then the distance from this projection to the apex should be laid off from the apex in the development on one of the corners of the pyramid between which is the trace from the apex to a and where a line drawn from this

Plate 19.

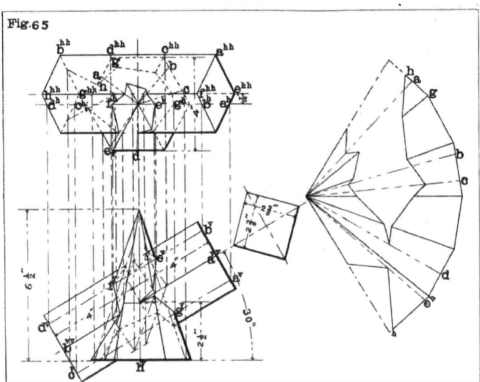

Fig. 65

point, and parallel with the base intersects the trace from the apex to a, will be the point sought.

By making projections from the remaining intersections of the corners of the prism with the pyramid and treating them in the manner already described, the remaining points in the development will be located, except the points h, and h. The length of g h, in the development is equal to g h, in the plan, and h h, is equal to v v.

Plate 20.

Fig. 66. If a circle is rolled on the outside of another circle, a point on its circumference will trace a curve which is called an epicycloid. If a circle is rolled on the inside of another circle, a point on its circumference will trace a curve which is called a hypocycloid. To describe these curves, draw the large circle as shown and a horizontal and vertical center line. Then, setting the spacing dividers to any distance, say $\frac{6}{16}$ of an inch, step this distance on the large circle, starting at the intersection of the vertical center line with the circumference, and step both ways. Be careful not to change the distance of the dividers. From the center of the large circle, draw the paths of the center of the small circles as a b c d. From the points laid off on the large circle draw radial lines as shown, and from where they intersect the path of the centers of the small circles as centers, and with radius equal to the radius of the small circles, draw arcs as shown. Now with the dividers at the same distance, step back on each arc from the points on the large circle as many times as the point numbers from the vertical center line. Then through the last points thus found draw the curve.

If a cord is kept taut while it is unwound from a cylinder, a point at its end will trace a curve which is called an involute. To describe an involute : With the spacing dividers set at about $\frac{6}{16}$ of an inch, step this distance on the large circle as shown. Be careful not to change the distance of the dividers. From these points draw radial lines and a perpendicular to each of these lines tangent to the points on the large circle. With the dividers at the same distance, step back on each tangent as many times as it is from the vertical center line. Through the last points thus found on each tangent, draw the curve.

Fig. 67. If a circle is rolled on a straight line, a point on its circumference will trace a curve which is called a cycloid. To describe the curve draw the straight line h h and lay off spaces the same as in Fig. 66. Through these points draw perpendiculars. A straight line through the center of the circle will be the path of the center. The intersection of this path with the perpendiculars will be centers from which to draw arcs with a radius equal to the radius of the circle. With the dividers at the same distance, step back on these arcs as many times as the arc is from a' a'. Through the last points on each arc thus found draw the curve.

These circles which we have been rolling are called generating circles, and are used to generate the curves of gear teeth. In good practice they are 1.9098 times the circular pitch in diameter, which is the length of an arc of the pitch circle from the center of one tooth to the center of the next tooth.

Plate 20.

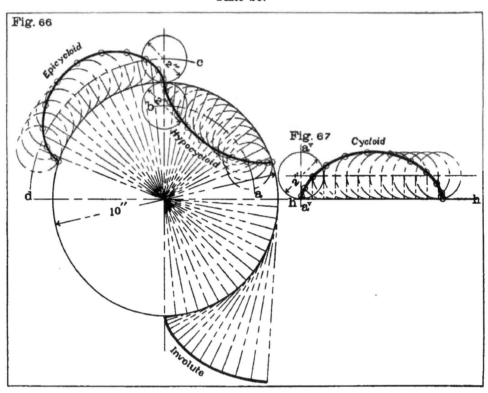

Fig. 66

Epicycloid

Hypocycloid

Involute

d

10"

a

c

p

Fig. 67

Cycloid

h

h

Plate 21.

CONVENTIONAL SCREW THREADS.

The bolt at the top of this plate is a drawing of a U. S. Standard bolt and nut, with the conventional thread. The sides of the thread known as the U. S. S. make an angle of 60° with each other, with a flat at the top and bottom of the thread equal to ⅛ of the pitch, and have a depth equal to .65 of the pitch. The pitch of a screw is that distance which it travels through the nut in one revolution. To lay out and draw this thread: First, draw the bolt in full (referring to table No. 5 for all dimensions not shown on the drawing) and lay off the depth of the thread and bisect it and draw what may be termed a pitch line as shown in the enlarged thread below the bolt; also draw a line at the root or bottom of the thread. Now it remains to determine the pitch, which is as follows: This bolt has 3½ threads per inch, and 3½ threads are equal to 7 threads in 2 inches, which is equal to ² pitch. The pitch being determined, lay off 2″ on the lower pitch line and divide into 14 equal parts, then each division will be equal to one-half of the pitch. Lay off as many more of these divisions as may be required for the number of threads on the bolt, and project each one of these points to the pitch line at the top of the bolt. Now with the 30° x 60° triangle with the shortest side to the T square, draw lines through alternate points on the lower pitch line, then in the opposite direction through the remaining points. The distance between the lines where they intersect the outside and root lines will be the width of the flat at top and bottom, which will be ⅛ of the pitch. Draw the top side in like manner, care being taken to have the outside of the thread directly opposite the root at the bottom side of the bolt, as shown. Having completed this, connect all points at top and bottom with straight lines as shown in the plate.

HEAD AND NUT.—The head and nut of the bolt are hexagonal prisms having the corners of the outside ends chamfered, or beveled, as shown.

The curves which are the result of this chamfer, are hyperbolas, formed by the sides of the head and nut intersecting a cone having the same axis as the bolt.

Draw a straight line on each side of the head, at an angle of 45 degrees. These lines should be drawn so as to intersect the end of the head in points, which have previously been located by drawing horizontal projecting lines tangent to the inscribing circle, which is shown in the end view. The nut is drawn in the same manner.

The bolt at the bottom of the plate represents the conventional square thread, the depth of which is equal to one-half of the pitch. Draw the outline of this screw, and lay off, on the top and bottom lines, divisions equal to one-half of the pitch, in this case, ½-inch. Now from the top and bottom side lay off the depth of the thread equal to one division, and through these points draw lines which will represent the root diameter, also lines through the points in the bottom side of the bolt, from the outside to the root both top and bottom. These lines will represent sides of the threads on the central plane and must be perpendicular to the axis of the bolt. Then connect each point in the top and bottom sides of the screw by straight lines, the first one at an inclination toward the left equal to one division, and draw all others parallel to this one. They represent the outside of the threads. Then at the same inclination in the opposite direction, draw the short lines on the left of the thread at the top, and on the right of the thread at the bottom, which will be an outline of a portion of the thread on the underside of the bolt. Now from where the lines forming the sides of the thread on the central plane intersect the lines forming the root diameter, draw lines to represent the root of the thread as shown. These are only drawn to the axis, because from this point on they could not be seen, and if drawn would be dotted, which is not desirable.

ACME SCREW THREAD.

degree screw thread, is known square thread, greater strength and superseding the latter. tion of 14½ degrees, angle, 29 degrees. The depth of the square inch, which is added for A. The width of the screw or tap thread

—The "ACME" or 29– superior to the well- and on account of its durability, is rapidly Each side has an inclina- which makes the included depth is the same as the thread, except .01 of an clearance. See C, Fig. point of tool for cutting

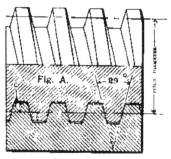

Plate 21.

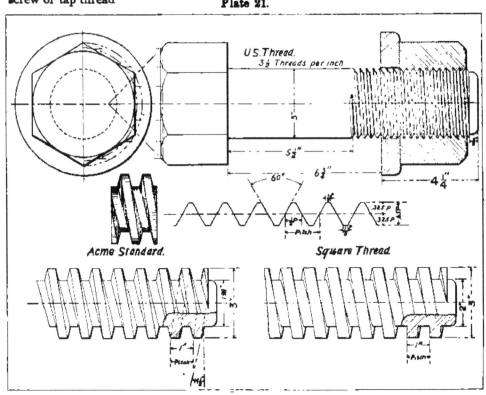

Acme Standard.   Square Thread.

$$= \frac{.3707}{\text{Number of threads per inch}} - .0052.$$

$$\text{Width of point of screw or nut thread} = \frac{.3707}{\text{Number of threads per inch}}$$

$$\text{Depth of thread of screw or nut} = \frac{.5}{\text{Number of threads per inch}} + .01$$

Diameter of screw at root of thread=Diameter of screw

$$- \left(\frac{1}{\text{Number of threads per inch}} + .02. \right)$$

$$\text{Pitch diameter} = \text{Diameter of screw} - \left(\frac{1}{\text{Number of threads per inch}} \right)$$

Draw the outline of this screw, and the pitch diameter as shown in Fig. A. Now, lay off on the pitch lines, the pitch, also the thickness of the threads equal to one-half of the pitch. From this point on, the work is similar to the United States Standard Thread and should be finished without any further instructions.

$$o = \frac{1}{4 \times \text{number of threads per inch}} \qquad N = o.$$

Plate 22.

THE HELIX.

If we suppose that the line a b is parallel to the axis of the cylinder, and a point moving along the line from a to b at a uniform velocity, while the cylinder makes one revolution about its axis at a uniform velocity, the point, if touching the cylinder, will trace a curve known as a helix. The distance a b will be what is termed the pitch of the helix. The pitch of a screw is equal to the axial distance through which the generating point travels in one revolution of the cylinder, both moving at uniform velocities. The helix may be drawn as follows : Draw a cylinder 4 inches in diameter, and 4 inches long, and divide the circumference of the cylinder in the top view into 12 equal parts, subdividing 4 of these into 3 equal parts as shown. Also divide the length of the cylinder into the same number of equal parts, and subdivide as is clearly shown in the plate. This may be done by drawing the straight line b h perpendicular to the axis of the cylinder, and in length equal to the circumference, laying off the distance at the top view on b h, and from each point drawing perpendiculars as shown. Also draw h a, which will be the development of the helix. Then by projecting the intersection of the perpendiculars with h a, as shown in the plate, the length of the cylinder will be properly divided. These traces intersected by projections from the top view, will locate the points through which to draw the helix a d b. The inner circle in the top view represents what is termed the "root cylinder" of a screw thread, the helix of which is drawn in the same manner as the above. From the projections in connection with the numbers there should be no difficulty in making this drawing. The angles shown in the plate are the angles which a tangent to the helices makes with the plane of the base of the pitch cylinders. The co-tangent of the angle is equal to the circumference of the cylinder divided by the pitch. The drawing of a quadruple square thread screw to the right of the top view gives the application of the helix to the screw thread.

This being a quadruple screw, means that the pitch is divided into four equal parts, each part being equal to one thread and one space, and is termed "individual pitch," and as the pitch of the helix is 4 inches, the individual pitch will be 1-inch. Make the thickness of the thread, the width of the space, and the depth, each equal to one-half of the individual pitch.

Then from a piece of thin wood make a curve to fit the helices from a to d and from c e, and with these draw the helices of the screw as clearly shown. This being a quadruple screw a thread at the top will be opposite a thread at the bottom.

Lay out and draw the nut with the same curves.

In drawing the helices of a screw it is well to use a bow pen to draw a small portion at the point of tangency, as at g.

The drawing at the lower side of the plate is to illustrate the method of drawing the thread usually used for a worm to work with a worm gear. The helices for this thread are determined in the same manner as explained above. To draw this thread, draw the outside, the pitch and root cylinders as shown at the right, and the outside, the pitch and root diameters in the front view. Then lay off on the pitch lines the pitch and thickness of the teeth equal to one-half of the pitch, and through these points draw the sides of all the teeth as shown in the section and the dotted outline at the bottom side. From the points where the sides of the teeth intersect the outside, the pitch and root cylinders, draw the outside, the pitch and root helices, then straight lines tangent to these helices, will be the visible contour of the thread in the finished drawing, instead of the straight lines drawn first through the pitch-points in the central plane. By referring to the view marked H, it will be noticed that these tangents at the right of the thread at the top extend to the point of tangency as at v, and only to the root on the left; at the bottom this will be reversed, as at h.

After the tool to cut this thread has been filed to the proper angle, file off the end of the tool until a gauge, as at a—which has a width equal to one-half of the pitch and a depth equal to .35 of the pitch—will touch the end and sides of the tool

Plate 22.

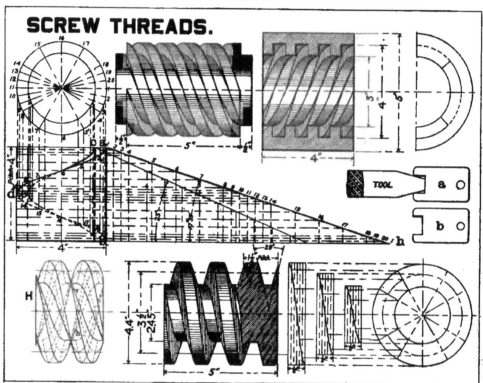

at the same time. It will then be the correct shape to form the thread, if the top side of the tool is in the same plane as the axis of the screw. When the thread is finished a gauge as at b should touch the top and sides of the thread at the same time. This gauge has a width equal to one-half of the pitch, with a depth equal to .3 of the pitch.

It is sometimes desirable to have parts of drawings representing curved surfaces shaded by drawing, straight or curved lines, parallel to each other.

In shading external surfaces, the lines should gradually increase, and the spaces decrease in width as they recede from the center line of the drawing, and the same as for internal surfaces.

Plate 22 A.

$$\text{Sine of angle G A C} = \frac{G\,B}{G\,A}$$

$$G\,B = G\,A \text{ x sine of angle G A C}$$

$$\text{Cosine of angle G A C} = \frac{A\,B}{G\,A}$$

$$A\,B = G\,A \text{ x cosine of angle G A C}$$

$$\text{Tangent of angle G A C} = \frac{G\,B}{A\,B}$$

$$H\,C = A\,C \text{ x tangent of angle G A C}$$

$$\text{Cotangent of angle G A C} = \frac{A\,B}{G\,B}$$

$$A\,C = H\,C \text{ x cotangent of angle G A C}$$

$$\text{Secant of angle G A C} = \frac{A\,C}{A\,B}$$

$$\text{Cosecant of angle G A C} = \frac{A\,C}{G\,B}$$

C i G, an arc of a circle.

A C, radius of a circle.

C G A, a sector.

A B, or E G, cosine of angle G A C.

G B, sine of angle G A C.

B C, versed sine of angle G A C.

C H, tangent of angle G A C.

D F, cotangent of angle G A C.

A H, secant of angle G A C.

A F, cosecant of angle G A C.

CIRCLE is a plain figure bounded by a curved line, or according to Locke's definition, "a line continued till it ends where it began, having all its parts equidistant from a common center."

The bounding line is called the circumference or periphery.

ARC is any part of the circumference of a circle.

CHORD is a right line joining the extremities of an arc.

SEGMENT OF A CIRCLE is any part bounded by an arc and its chord.

RADIUS OF A CIRCLE is a line drawn from the center of a circle to the circumference.

SECTOR is any part of a circle bounded by an arc and its two radii.

SEMI-CIRCLE is half a circle.

QUADRANT is a quarter of a circle.

SECANT is a line running from the center of a circle to extremity of tangent of arc.

COSECANT is secant of complement of arc.

SINE is a line running from one extremity of an arc perpendicular to a diameter passing through the other extremity.

VERSED SINE is that part of the diameter intercepted between sine and arc.

COSINE is that part of the diameter intercepted between sine and center.

TANGENT is a right line that touches a circle without cutting it.

COTANGENT is tangent of complement of arc.

THE CIRCUMFERENCE OF A CIRCLE is supposed to be divided into 360 equal parts, termed degrees; each degree into 60 minutes and each minute into 60 seconds.

COMPLEMEMT OF AN ANGLE is what remains after subtracting angle from 90 degrees.

Plate 22 A.

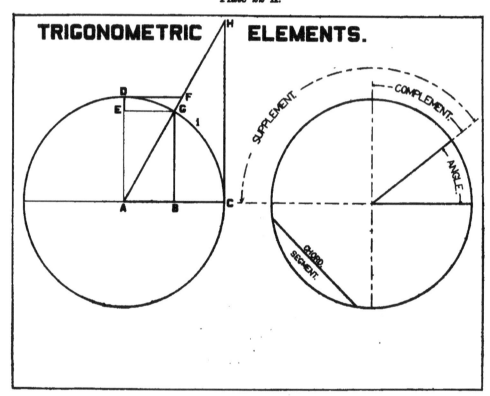

SUPPLEMENT OF ANGLE is what remains after subtracting angle from 180 degrees.

PLANE.—A plane is a surface without curvature, or according to Euclid, "it is such a surface that if any two points whatever in it be joined by a straight line, the whole of the straight line will be in the same surface. In conic sections, and all solid bodies, it signifies an imaginary surface supposed to cut and pass through them. In fact, the whole doctrine of conic sections is based on this foundation.

Plate 23.

SPUR-GEARING.

When motion is transmitted from one shaft to another, the axes of which are parallel, toothed gears are used, the pitch surfaces of which are imaginary cylinders. Let two perfect cylinders be keyed fast on shafts whose axes are parallel and such a distance apart that the cylinders are in contact. Then if one cylinder revolves the other will revolve also, and if there is no slipping the two cylinders will have equal velocities at the point of contact. On these cylinders is laid off the pitch, which is the distance from the centre of one tooth to the centre of the next, measured along the pitch-circle. It is termed circular pitch. The addendum is generally .3 of the circular pitch, and the space below .35 of the circular pitch, making a total depth of .65 of the circular pitch. The diameter of the pitch-circle is equal to the number of teeth multiplied by the pitch, and this product by .3183. Then pitch diameter = number of teeth × pitch × .3183. Outside diameter equals pitch diameter plus .6 of the pitch, and the root diameter equals pitch diameter minus .7 of the pitch. The radii of these circles are equal to the diameters divided by 2.

Diametral Pitch.—If a gear has 48 teeth and 6 inches pitch diameter, it is 8 pitch. That is, for each inch of the pitch diameter there are 8 teeth in the circumference. Then

$$\text{Pitch} = \frac{\text{number of teeth}}{\text{pitch diameter}} \text{ and}$$

$$\text{Pitch diameter} = \frac{\text{number of teeth}}{\text{pitch}}$$

$$\text{Number of teeth} = \text{pitch diameter} \times \text{pitch}$$

$$\text{The addendum} = \frac{1}{\text{diametral pitch}}$$

$$\text{Then whole diameter} = \frac{\text{number of teeth} + 2}{\text{diametral pitch}}$$

$$\text{Whole depth of the teeth} = \frac{2.15708}{\text{diametral pitch}}$$

Pitch = 8. Number of teeth = 48, then $\frac{48}{8} = 6$ inches pitch diameter.

$$\text{And } \frac{48}{6} = 8 \text{ pitch.}$$

$$\text{And outside diameter} = \frac{48 + 2}{8} = 6\frac{1}{4} \text{ inches.}$$

Involute Gearing.—Compute the diameters as explained for circular pitch, and lay off on the pitch-circles of the gear and pinion the pitch, also the thickness of the teeth equal to one-half of the circular pitch. Then draw through c a straight line making an angle of 14½° with the centre line, and perpendicular to this line draw the line of action through the pitch-point p. The intersections of these two lines will locate the point b. With c as a centre and radius c b draw base circle as shown, and divide b p into say five equal parts. Then starting at b, lay these same parts off on the base circle toward the left. The last point will fall a little to the left of the centre line. Also mark off four or five times from b toward the right. Lay the dividers down carefully so that their distance will not be changed. From these points draw radial lines and perpendicular to each of these, tangent to the

60

points on the base circle. With the dividers, which have not been changed, step
back on each tangent as many times as it numbers from p. Through the last point
on each tangent thus found draw the involute, which does not extend below the base
circle. Find by trial, centres from which face and flank-curves can be drawn, then
through these centres draw circles: which will be circles of centres from which all
the curves may be drawn with the same radius. The flanks below the base circle
will be radial lines. The radius for the fillet is equal to the product of the constant
number for 30 teeth in column No. 5, table No. 3, multiplied by the pitch. The
involute for the pinion is drawn in the same manner. The flanks of the teeth are
drawn from the base circle tangent to the circle at the centre, the radius of which

Plate 23.

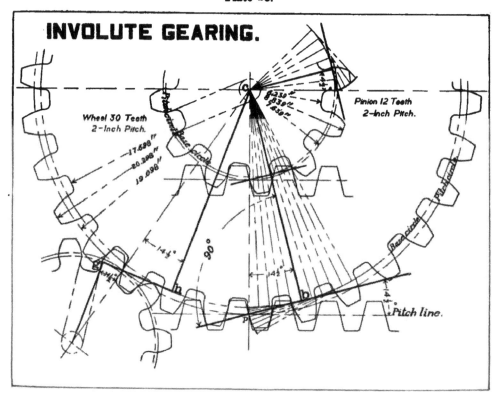

is equal to the product of the constant number for 12 teeth, column 4, table No. 3,
multiplied by the pitch. Draw a few teeth of the pinion in gear with the gear as
shown at the left hand corner at the bottom. Also the line of action as shown by
the heavy lines. The straight line g h represents the flexible cord, which being
unwound from the base circles, generates the involutes. This line is also the path
of contact of the teeth, that is the teeth are in contact with each other along this
straight line. The rack is a gear with an infinite number of teeth; the involutes
of the flanks are straight lines through the pitch-points, perpendicular to the line of
action, that is 14½° in opposite directions. The faces of the teeth are drawn with
a radius equal to the product of the pitch and the constant number for 150 teeth,
column 2, table No. 3, laid off from the pitch-point p on the line of action produced.

Plate 24.

APPROXIMATE INVOLUTE TEETH.

Compute the pitch, the outside and root diameters of the gear and pinion as explained in plate 23, and draw the line of action at $14\frac{1}{2}°$, which may be done as follows: b c is equal to the cosine of $14\frac{1}{2}°$, and p b is equal to the sine of $14\frac{1}{2}°$. As .96815. $=$ cosine of $14\frac{1}{2}°$ and .25038 $=$ sine of $14\frac{1}{2}°$, p c $\times$ .96815 $=$ b c, and p c $\times$ .25038 $=$ p b. This is for $14\frac{1}{2}°$ only. For $20°$ it will be p c $\times$.93969 $=$ b c, and p c $\times$ .34202 $=$ p b, and this can only be used for $20°$. The angle of action being drawn, lay off the pitch, and thickness of teeth equal to one-half of the pitch. The gear has 30 teeth and is 2 inches pitch: find in table 3, column 2, opposite 30 teeth, the constant number, 1.4079, which, multiplied by the pitch, will give the radius with which to draw the face of the teeth. This radius must be laid off on the line of action from the pitch-point p toward g^r and will give the centre from which to draw the face of the teeth, as p v. Through this centre draw a circle which will be a circle of centres from which to draw the remainder of the teeth. Find in table 3, column 3, opposite 30 teeth, the constant number .990, which, multiplied by the pitch, will give the radius for the flanks of the teeth from the pitch-circle to the base circle. This laid off on the line of action from the pitch-point p toward b will give the centre from which to draw the flanks. Then a circle through this centre will be a circle of centres from which to draw the remainder of the teeth. The teeth of the pinion are drawn in the same manner, as the gear. By referring to the table and taking the constant number opposite the number of the teeth desired, a gear having any number of teeth may be drawn, the teeth of which will be as accurate as the average teeth in actual practice. The rack teeth are drawn in the same manner as in plate 23. The object in rounding the face of the rack teeth is to make them interchangeable with a 12-tooth pinion. The space between the teeth of a 12-tooth pinion below the base circle is almost parallel, being just a trifle wider at the base circle than at the root circle. This is done to facilitate matters in cutting the teeth, and also adds some strength to the teeth. If the flanks below the base circle were made so that the rack teeth would work without rounding the face, (which should not be done), then the space between the pinion teeth would be wider at the root than at the base circle, which would complicate matters in cutting the teeth and also weaken the teeth. Drawing the teeth as they are, not only necessitates the rounding of the faces of rack teeth but all gears of 150 teeth and over must be drawn with the radius for 150 teeth. By increasing the angle of action to $20°$ or more this is overcome, allowing all the gear teeth to be true involutes, and the sides of the rack teeth straight lines, as they should be, but for the reason already explained.

Plate 24.

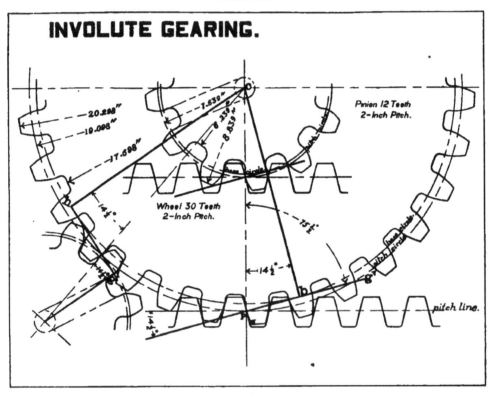

Plate 25.

CYCLOIDAL GEAR TEETH.

As already explained in plate 20, if a circle rolls on the outside of a circle, a fixed point on its circumference will generate an epicycloid, which being on the outside of the circle will be the curve which must be used for the faces of the teeth. If a circle rolls on the inside of a circle, a fixed point on its circumference will generate a hypocycloid, which, being on the inside of the circle, will be the curve which must be used for the flanks of the teeth. And if a circle rolls on a straight line, a fixed point on its circumference will generate a cycloid, which will be the curve for the face and flank of the rack teeth. Compute and draw the pitch, the outside and root circles for a pinion having 12 teeth and a gear having 30 teeth 1½ inches pitch, also the pitch the outside and root lines for the racks as shown in the plate. Then draw the generating circles tangent to the pitch-circles at the pitch-points p and p, and, using the pitch-point p as the fixed point on the generating circles, generate the curves as explained in plate 20.

The diameters of the generating circles are equal to half the pitch diameter of the pinion, which will make them equal to 1.9098 times the pitch Then the diameter of the generating circle for a gear of any pitch, is equal to 1.9098 × pitch. The curves for the rack teeth are generated in the same manner as the cycloid in plate 20. All the curves being generated, lay off the pitch, and the thickness of the teeth equal to half the pitch, and find centres to approximate these curves, and through these centres draw circles, which will be circles of centres from which to draw the curves of the teeth. The path of contact is represented by the heavy arcs a p, p b, that is as the gear roll the teeth are in contact along these arcs. By multiplying the proportional figures in the plate, by the pitch, the different proportions of the gear may be obtained. Thus .625 p means that the thickness of the rim below the root circle is equal to .625 × pitch, and the rest in like manner. The width of the arms is equal to 1.625 times the pitch at the pitch-circle, and enlarged toward the centre .75 in 12 inches. The thickness of the arms at the pitch-circle is equal to .4 of the pitch, and is enlarged toward the centre .75 in 12 inches. A normal section of the arms should be an ellipse. The radius of the fillets at the root of the teeth may be equal to .05 of the pitch.

Plate 25.

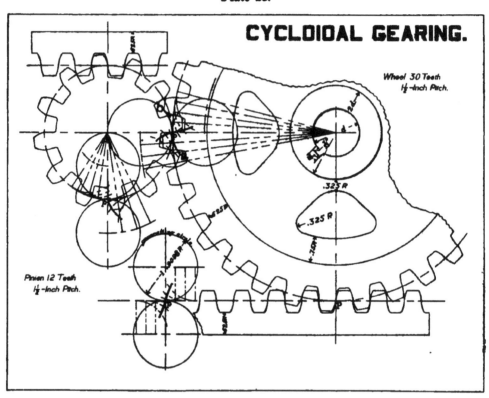

CYCLOIDAL GEARING.

Plate 26.

BEVEL GEARING.

It will be readily understood from what has already been said about spur-gearing that when motion is transmitted from one shaft to another by such gearing, the shafts must be parallel to each other. When shafts are so situated that the axes of the shafts are in the same plane and at right angles to each other, they will, if produced, intersect each other. Motion is transmitted by gears whose pitch surfaces are cones, instead of cylinders. They are known as bevel gears, if the cones are unequal; and as mitre gears, if the cones are equal. To draw the bevel gear: First draw the axes at right angles to each other; and lay off from the intersection of the axes at o on the axis of the pinion the pitch-radius of the gear, as o b; and the pitch-radius of the pinion on the axis of the gear, as o h. Now draw lines through b and h until they intersect in g and make b b' equal to b g; also h h' equal to h g. Then g b' will be the pitch diameter of the pinion; and g h' the pitch diameter of the gear. From the points g b' and h' draw lines to the point o. The angle g o h is the centre angle of the gear; and g o b the centre angle of the pinion. These angles may be found as follows: When the shafts are at right angles to each other only, divide the number of teeth in gear by the number of teeth in pinion, which will give the tangent of the centre angle of gear. This angle, subtracted from 90°, will give the centre angle of the pinion. Now through the points g b' and h' draw lines perpendicular to g o, b' o and h' o, and produce them until they intersect the axis as at o' and g'. These lines will represent the normal cones to the pitch cones o h' g and o g b'. Lay off on these perpendiculars as shown at h' the addendum, and depth below—which is the same as in spur-gearing—and from these points draw lines to o. Then lay off the length of the teeth, 2 inches, and draw lines through these points parallel with the lines forming the outside end of the teeth. If these normal cones be developed, the base of each one will be an arc of a circle. The centre of one is o' and radius o' g; and of the other the centre is g' and radius g' g. Now produce o g as to h', and from o' and g' draw lines parallel to o g h'. Then at any convenient distance draw c c' parallel to o' g'. It is here we develop the outline of the teeth. Draw the line of action at an angle of 20°. Now with c as a centre and radius c p draw arc of pitch-circle, and with the same centre and radii found in the same manner as c p draw addendum and root circles. The pinion is treated in like manner. Lay off the pitch and thickness of teeth and proceed exactly the same as for spur-gearing, with the exception of one thing, which is the number of teeth from which to select the tabular number for the faces and flanks of the teeth. h g is the true pitch-radius of this gear having 18 teeth of 1″ pitch; but the teeth are laid out on an arc of a circle of a much larger radius, which is c p. Then a gear of radius c p will contain 1″ pitch more than 18 times. Therefore, we must select a tabular number for a gear of a greater number of teeth than 18. And also a cutter to cut the gear for a greater number than 18. This is determined as follows: Multiply c p by 6.28 and divide by circular pitch, then we have:

$$\text{Number of teeth} = \frac{6\,28 \times c\,p}{\text{circular pitch}}$$

Use tabular number in table No. 1, 20° line of action and proceed in the same manner as for 14½°. The thickness for the small end of the teeth is shown on the arc v v, the radius of which is equal to r v. This pitch is also equal to the product of the pitch at the large end and the quotient of o g into o v. The teeth at the small end are drawn in the same manner as at the large end. The same tabular numbers must be multiplied by the pitch on the arc **v v.**

To draw the view at the left : Project from the section of the pinion as indicated, and through these points draw the pitch, the outside and the root circles. Next lay off the pitch as many times as there are teeth in the pinion ; also the thickness of the teeth, equal to one-half the pitch. Now make projection from the small end of the teeth in the sectional view, in the same manner as from the large end, which will give points through which the pitch, the outside and the root circles of the small end will pass.

Plate 26.

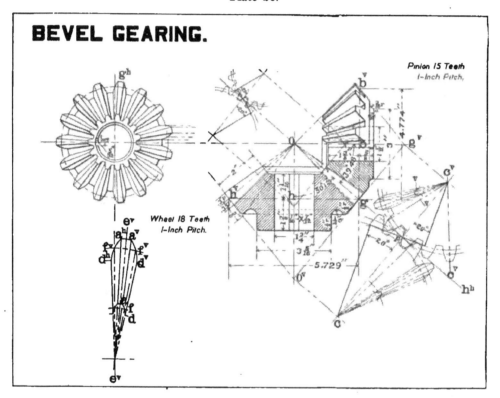

BEVEL GEARING.

Pinion 15 Teeth
1-Inch Pitch.

Wheel 18 Teeth
1-Inch Pitch.

To draw the outlines of these teeth : Draw one tooth as at g^h, from the following explanation of the enlarged tooth below. Bisect the arc f^v f^v with the radial line e^v e^v, and make the distance each side of e^v e^v on the outside, the pitch and the root circles equal to the distance each side of c^v c^v. Through these points draw the outlines a^v f^v d^v ; a^h f^v d^h. Then where radial lines through these points intersect the circles at the small end of the teeth, will be points through which the outline of the small end of the teeth will pass, as indicated on one side by a f d, and also the outside and root of the teeth as a^v a and d^v d. Find, by trial, centers from which arcs can be drawn through a^v f^v d^v and a f d, then circles drawn through these centers will give circles of centers from which the remaining teeth can be drawn through the pitch-points. All elements of the teeth of bevel gears must run to the vertex o, of the pitch cone, whatever may be the angles of the shafts to each other. The teeth in the upper half of the pinion are drawn as indicated by the projection.

67

Plate 27.
WORM AND WORM-WHEEL.

This gearing is employed when the shafts cross each other but do not intersect, and may be considered as a spur-gear and rack; that is a section on the central plane b b is the same as a rack and spur-gear, having the same pitch and number of teeth. Therefore draw the pitch-circle of the gear; and tangent to it at the pitch-point p draw pitch-line which may be considered as the pitch-line of a rack to work with the gear. From this pitch-line lay off the pitch diameter of the worm 3.375". Draw the outside and root diameter of the gear and worm in the manner instructed in plates 22 and 23. Next, draw the line of action as shown, and generate the involute in the manner already explained, and divide the pitch-circle into as many equal spaces as there are teeth, and lay off the thickness of the teeth equal to one-half of the pitch, and draw the outline of the teeth as clearly shown in the section.

It now remains to determine the contour and its limits at the edge or end of the teeth, which may be done as follows: From where a h intersects the outside, the pitch and the root cylinders of the worm, project to the corresponding helices as shown by the dotted outline in the front view. This will give a foreshortened outline of the worm thread space as shown. Produce a h to the axis of the gear as at g', draw a' g parallel to a g', and project c to c'; also the intersection of the outside and root cylinder with a h, which will give the limit of the worm thread space above and below the pitch-line c c'. Then lay off the outline of the section in the same relation to c' g as the outline of the section in the front view is to p d; this will be a parallel view of the worm thread space. Transfer this view to an extra piece of paper as shown at p g^h, lay off on the pitch-line equal divisions each side of p, also the same divisions on the axis of the wheel the same number of times each side of g^h. With g^h p as a radius and the points on the axis each side of g^h as centers, draw arcs tangent to each point on the pitch-line as shown, which will represent the pitch-circle in different positions as it rolls on the pitch-line of the worm. Then on a piece of tracing cloth draw the pitch-line of the worm and perpendicular to it a line equal to p g^h, with p g^h as a radius, and g^h as a center, draw an arc of the pitch-circle through p; on this arc of the pitch-circle lay off divisions equal to those on the drawing. Place the tracing on the drawing so that p and g^h on the tracing coincides with p g^h on the drawing, fasten with thumb tacks and trace the section, remove the tacks and revolve the tracing until the pitch-circle on the tracing coincides with the next arc of the pitch-circle on the drawing, and the next point to p on the tracing coincides with the next point on the pitch-line, fasten with the thumb tacks and trace the section again. Repeat this four or five times in each direction, then the envelope of these tracings will be the contour of the gear tooth, on the parallel plane, as seen in the parallel view at c'. Find centers from which this outline can be drawn and transfer it from the tracing to the parallel view, in the same relation to c' g, as it is to p g^h on the tracing. By projecting from the sectional view as shown at the top, the radii of the circles which limit the curves of the teeth at the outside and bottom will be obtained. These circles having been drawn, lay off on these circles and the pitch-circle the points through which to draw the left outline of a tooth in the same relation to p d as they are to a' g in the parallel view, then by making the width at the outside, the pitch, and the bottom equal to the width at the corresponding circles in the parallel view, will give the points through which to draw the other side of the tooth. Then by drawing these outlines in the same relation to all the pitch-points the front side of the teeth are finished. The outlines of the rear side are found in the same manner, by first finding an outline of the worm thread space on the rear side of the same space. In drawing these

Plate 27.

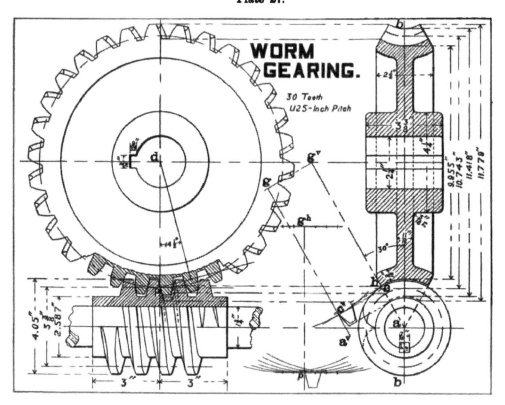

arcs upon which to place the tracing cloth, the longer they are the better for accuracy. This is a very difficult operation, therefore great care should be exercised. The outside diameter of the gear may be determined as follows: The radius of the root cylinder plus the clearance multiplied by the versed sine of 30°, and this product multiplied by 2, then this last product added to what would be the outside diameter of a spur-gear having the same number of teeth and pitch, will give outside diameter of the worm-gear. Versed sin. of 30° = .13397

Plate 28.

When the path of contact, A B, of the teeth of gears is in a straight line, which is inclined to the line of centers, the form of the teeth is an involute of a circle concentric to the pitch-circle, and has the path of contact for a tangent.

Draw the pitch-circles of three pairs of 12–tooth gears of 1.5 diametral pitch. Lay off the line of action of each pair as shown in the plate. Next, draw the base circle of each gear marked E, through the points marked B, and the base circle of each gear marked D, through the points marked A. Now, draw the addendum circle of each gear marked D, through the points marked B, and the addendum circle of each gear marked E, through the points marked A. The addendum of the gears in Fig. A, is .3099 of the circular pitch, 2.0944 inches, of the gear in Fig. B, .1718 of the circular pitch, 2.0944 inches, of the gear in Fig. C, .3994 of the circular pitch, 2.0944 inches. The dedendum in each case is .05 of the circular pitch greater than the addendum.

Let the flexible, but non-elastic, band H F, be secured to the base circles at H and F, of each pair of gears. Now, if the gears marked D, be revolved as indicated by the arrows, the band will be wound on the gears marked E, and unwound from the gears marked D, and at the same time cause the gears marked E, to revolve as indicated by the arrows. And, while the gears are revolving, a tracing point secured to the band at each point marked A, will move along the line A P B, which is tangent to the base circles at the points marked A and B. During this movement of the tracing point along the line A P B, it will trace the involutes A G and A C. The contact of the teeth begins at A, and ends at B; and as the addendum circles are drawn through A and B, the full length of contact is used. The addendum is usually .3 to .31416 of the circular pitch. If the pitch is

diametral, the addendum is usually $\dfrac{1}{\text{Diametral pitch}} = .31416$ of the circular pitch,

or a trifle more than .3 of the circular pitch. The figures show contours of the teeth at the beginning and ending of contact, also at the pitch-point and other intermediate points. Furthermore, the point of contact of each pair of contours lies in the straight line A P B. The flank of the driving tooth acts upon the face of the driven tooth during the first part of the action, from A to P, and the face of the driving tooth acts upon the flank of the driven tooth during the last part of the action, from P to B. The arcs of the pitch-circles from the pitch-point P, to the contours A G and A C, are called the arcs of approach, and the arcs from the pitch-point P, to the contours J B and I B, are called the arcs of recess. The arc from the contour A G, to the contour J B, and the arc from the contour A C, to the contour I B, are called the arcs of action; and that one pair of teeth may not go out of gear before another pair comes into gear, these arcs of action should not be less than 1.5 times the circular pitch. We have in Fig. B, a drawing of a pair of 12–tooth gears of 1.5 diametral pitch and an angle of action of 14½ degrees. It also shows that the arcs of action are not greater than the circular-pitch; and as has already been stated an addendum of only .1718 of the circular pitch. By increasing the angle of action to 20 degrees we get an arc of action of a greater length, and an addendum of .3099 of the circular pitch, and by going to 23 degrees we get an arc of action very near to that which is required, and an addendum greater than is required. Assuming 12 teeth to be the least number of teeth in a gear, and an addendum of .3 or .31416 of the circular pitch, it can be seen at a glance that 20 or 23 degrees is the most advantageous angle of action. Again, if we draw a horizontal line through each point marked A, also through each point marked B, the distance from P, to where each line intersects the line of centers will be the addendum of the rack—which is less than the addendum of the gear.

Plate 28.

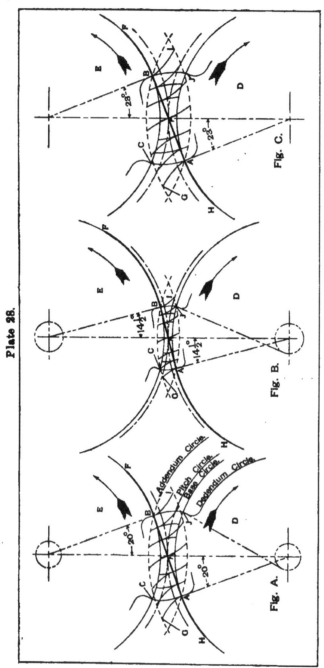

Fig. A.

Fig. B.

Fig. C.

The addendum of the rack when the angle of action is 20 degrees is .2 23 of the circular pitch ; when the angle of action is 14½ degrees the addendum is .1197 of the circular pitch ; when the angle of action is 23 degrees the addendum is .291 of the circular pitch, nearly .3. Therefore when a 12-tooth gear is used as the smallest gear of the system, and .3 or .31416 of the circular pitch as an addendum, less than 23 degrees should not be used.

The reason for using 14½ degrees almost exclusively in the work of this book is this : The manufacturers of cutters for cutting the teeth of gears usually make them for 14½ degrees ; and many who make a specialty of gear-cutting use the same angle. One great objection to using an angle greater than 14½ degrees is the increased journal friction, which increases as the angle of action increases. Admitting that an increase from 14½ to 23 degrees does increase journal friction ; it may be safely said that the increase of friction by the use of a wrench in the hands of an incompetent or careless workman, far exceeds that produced by an increase of the angle of action.

GEAR FORMULA.

C = circular pitch.
O = outside diameter of gear.
n = number of teeth in gear.
p = diametral pitch.
p' = pitch diameter of gear.
r = root diameter of gear.
h = whole depth of teeth.
t = thickness of tooth at pitch-circle.

$$p' = \frac{n}{p}$$

$$p = \frac{n}{p'}$$

$$p = \frac{n + 2}{O}$$

If 2 be added to the number of teeth of a gear, and the sum be divided by the diametral pitch, the quotient will be the outside diameter of the gear.

$$O = \frac{n + 2}{p}$$

If 2.31416 be subtracted from the number of teeth in a gear and the remainder be divided by the diametral pitch, the quotient will be the root diameter.

$$r = \frac{n - 2.31416}{p}$$

Then if 2.31416 be subtracted from the number of teeth in a gear and the remainder be divided by the root diameter, the diametral pitch will be obtained.

$$p = \frac{n - 2.31416}{r}$$

$$t = \frac{1.5708}{p} = .5 \times \text{circular pitch}$$

$$h = \frac{2.15708}{p} = .686 \times \text{circular pitch}$$

$$C = \frac{3.1416}{p}$$

$$p = \frac{3.1416}{O}$$

The circumference of a circle multiplied by .3183 equals diameter of the circle.
The circumference of a circle multiplied by .1591545 equals radius of the circle.
If the addendum of a gear tooth is .3 of the circular pitch, the diametral pitch may be obtained by adding 1.88496 to the number of teeth and dividing the sum by the outside diameter of the gear.

$$p = \frac{n + 1.88496}{O}$$

Then if 1.88496 be added to the number of teeth in a gear, and the sum be divided by the diametral pitch, the quotient will be the outside diameter.

$$O = \frac{n + 1.88496}{p}$$

If the depth below the pitch-circle is .35 of the circular pitch, the diametral pitch may be obtained by subtracting 2.19912 from the number of teeth in the gear, and dividing the remainder by the root diameter.

$$p = \frac{n - 2.19912}{r}$$

Then if 2.19912 be subtracted from the number of teeth in a gear, and the remainder be divided by the diametral pitch, the quotient will be the root diameter of the gear.

$$r = \frac{n - 2.19912}{p}$$

When the addendum of a gear is .3 of the circular pitch, and the whole depth of the teeth is .65 of the circular pitch, the whole depth of the tooth may be obtained by dividing 2.04204 by the diametral pitch.

$$h = \frac{2.04204}{p}$$

The pupil may ask himself why does 3.1416 divided by the diametral pitch give the circular pitch. The diametral pitch as already explained, is a certain number of teeth in the circumference of the pitch-diameter, to each inch of the pitch-diameter. For example, suppose a gear is 4 pitch, there are 4 teeth in the circumference for each inch of the pitch-diameter. If the gear has 4 teeth it is 1 inch pitch-diameter; if it has 8 teeth it is 2 inches pitch-diameter; if it has 12 teeth it is 3 inches pitch-diameter. If a gear is 5 pitch, and has 5 teeth it is 1 inch pitch-diameter; if it contains 10 teeth it is 2 inches pitch-diameter; and so on for any pitch or number of teeth.

If the circumference of the pitch-diameter of a gear be divided by the number of teeth in the gear the circular pitch will be obtained. Then if a gear is 4 pitch and contains 4 teeth, the pitch-diameter is 1 inch, and the circumference is 3.1416 inches the circumference of a circle being 3.1416 times the diameter. Again if a gear is 4 pitch and contains 24 teeth, the pitch-diameter is 6 inches, and the circumference is 18.8496 inches, or 3.1416 × 6.

$$\text{Then } \frac{3.1416}{4} = \frac{18.8496}{24}$$

$$\text{Then } \frac{3.1416}{\text{diametral pitch}} = \text{circular pitch}$$

$$\text{And } \frac{3.1416}{\text{circular pitch}} = \text{diametral pitch.}$$

Plate 29 is an illustration of the above.

Let us take what may be considered the worst case of a gear, from which we want to obtain the diametral pitch, the pitch diameter, the outside diameter, and the circular pitch. Suppose we have an old gear that has every tooth broken off, and nothing remains except the marks where the teeth were. Say there are 40 of them, which means there had been 40 teeth in the gear. Measure the root diameter, which we find to be 7.537 + inches. We are now ready to obtain the diametral pitch, the pitch-diameter, the outside diameter, and the circular pitch.

$$p = \frac{n - 2.31416}{7.537 +}$$

$$p' = \frac{n}{p}$$

$$O = \frac{n + 2}{p}$$

$$C = \frac{3.1416}{p}$$

Plate 29.

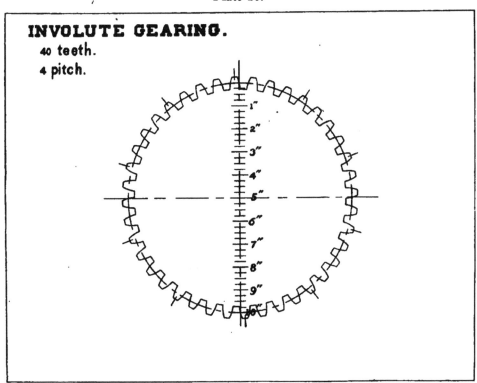

INVOLUTE GEARING.

40 teeth.

4 pitch.

Plate 30.
SPIRAL GEARING.

The spiral gear is unlike the spur-gears in plates 23, 24 and 25; because the teeth of a spiral gear are not cut in a straight line, but are like a screw, helical. In plate 22 we have an example of a quadruple screw of 4-inch pitch. This pitch is divided into 4 equal parts, which makes 4 teeth on the end of the screw. Therefore, the spiral gear may be considered to be a cylinder having a number of spiral grooves of a coarse pitch. If it is required to make a spiral gear of 20 teeth, the cylinder must have 20 spirals. There is no great difficulty in drawing the spiral gear if it is known how to generate the spiral, heretofore known as a helix. As already explained, the pitch of a spiral or helix, is the axial distance through which the generating point moves in one revolution of the cylinder. This we will term axial pitch. Referring to the plate, it will be noticed that the axial pitch is 9 inches, and the distance f g, which is supposed to be the thickness of the gear, is only 2 inches.

The problem is to generate that portion of the helix or spiral from e to i. In doing this, the divisions between f and g, are the only divisions used; as the divisions to the right of f, and to the left of g, are there for illustration.

This cylinder is 10 inches diameter, and will be considered as the pitch diameter of a gear. The circumference is divided into 36 equal parts, 10 degrees each. We are now ready to determine the width of the spaces between f and g, which may be done by the following proportion : $360 : 10 :: 9 : x = \dfrac{10 \times 9}{360} = .25$-inch, which is the width of each space between f and g. This must be done : because one division between f and g, must be the same to the axial pitch of the spiral, as one division in the circle is to the circumference of the circle. And the arc a b v, has the same number of divisions as the distance between f and g. And the arc a b v, is the same to the circumference of the circle, as the distance between f and g is to 9 inches.

We are now ready to make this drawing, which may be done as follows : Draw the circle, making it 10 inches diameter, which is understood to be the pitch diameter of a gear, and divide it into 36 equal parts. Lay off f g equal to 2 inches, and divide it into 8 equal parts for the reason already explained. Project the point a to e, and all other points between a v, as shown, and draw the spiral from e to i through the points located by projection.

Now put in the divisions to the right of f, and to the left of g, and finish the spiral. Make c d=1¼ inches, and draw c n parallel to e i.

In drawing the spiral gear we must consider the normal pitch, the actual pitch and the angle which the spiral makes with the axis of the gear, known as the spiral angle. To obtain the spiral angle when the axial pitch is given : Divide the circumference of the pitch cylinder by the axial pitch, the quotient will be the tangent of the angle which the spiral makes with the axis of the gear.

The normal circular pitch is measured normal to the spiral, as the line c d, and is equal to the actual circular pitch multiplied by the cosine of the spiral angle. The actual circular pitch is the distance from the center of one tooth to the center of the next, measured on the pitch-circle, as the arc a b, in the same manner as explained for plate 23, and is equal to the normal circular pitch divided by the cosine of the spiral angle.

Plate 30.

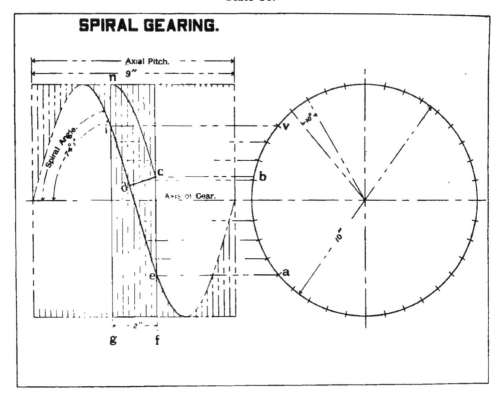

$$\text{Actual circular pitch} = \frac{\text{Normal circular pitch}}{\text{Cosine of the spiral angle}}$$

Normal circular pitch=Actual circular pitch multiplied by cosine of spiral angle.

Actual diametral pitch=Normal diametral pitch multiplied by cosine of spiral angle.

$$\text{Normal diametral pitch} = \frac{\text{Actual diametral pitch}}{\text{Cosine of spiral angle}}$$

Plate 31.

The curvature of the teeth of a spiral gear is not the same the curvature of the teeth of a spur-gear which has the same number of teeth and pitch ; but is the same as the curvature of the teeth of a spur-gear of a larger diameter, and a greater number of teeth, which have the same pitch as the normal pitch of the spiral gear. The number of teeth of the spur-gear, according to Mr. George B. Grant, is found in the following manner :

$$\frac{\text{Actual number of teeth}}{\text{Cosine of spiral angle}}\ 3$$

Assuming a spiral gear to have 30 teeth, we have $\dfrac{30}{.7071}\ 3 = 85$ nearly,

which is near enough for all practical purposes.

Now, $\dfrac{85}{4} = 21\frac{1}{4}$ inches, pitch diameter, and $21\frac{1}{4} \div 2 = 10\frac{5}{8}$ inches, radius of pitch diameter. With g as a center, and a radius of $10\frac{5}{8}$ inches, draw the arc j k. The addendum is equal to $\dfrac{1}{\text{Normal diametral pitch}} = \frac{1}{4} = \frac{1}{4}$-inch. With g as a center, and a radius of $10\frac{5}{8} + \frac{1}{4} = 10\frac{7}{8}$ inches, draw the addendum circle. The depth of the teeth is equal to $\dfrac{2.15708}{\text{Normal diametral pitch}} = \dfrac{2.15708}{4} = .53927.$ With g as a center, and a radius of $10\frac{7}{8} - .53927 = 10.336$ inches, draw the dedendum circle. Lay off and draw a few teeth, as shown. Now draw the line g v, so as to bisect one of the teeth, as shown. Next, draw n o, perpendicular to g v, also, the line a b, at the same angle to n o, as the spiral is to the axis of the gear, in this case, 45 degrees. From v, the intersection of these lines, draw another line perpendicular to a b, and at any convenient point on the line, as at f, as a center, and 5.304 inches as a radius, draw an arc of the pitch-circle of the 30–tooth gear.

(1) Diameter of pitch-circle $= \dfrac{\text{Actual number of teeth}}{\text{Actual diametral pitch}} = \dfrac{30}{2.828} = 5.304.$

(2) The addendum is equal to $\dfrac{1}{\text{Normal diametral pitch}} = \frac{1}{4} = .25$-inch.

(3) Whole depth of teeth is equal to $\dfrac{2.15708}{\text{Normal diametral pitch}} = \dfrac{2.15708}{4} =$

.53927. Now, draw the addendum and dedendum circles, and make projections as indicated.

Plate 32.

This drawing shows a pair of spiral gears having respectively 30 and 25 teeth, of 4 normal pitch, and 2.828 actual pitch.

The spiral angle of each gear is 45 degrees.

The axial pitch of the 30–tooth gear is 33.326 inches, and the 25–tooth gear has an axial pitch of 27.772 inches.

Axial pitch $= \dfrac{\text{Circumference of pitch-circle}}{\text{Tangent of spiral angle}}$ The spiral of the 30–tooth gear is right–hand, and of the 25–tooth gear, left–hand. Draw the pitch, addendum and dedendum circles to the dimensions shown, and lay off the actual circular pitch and thickness of the teeth. See formulas 1, 2 and 3. We are now ready to transfer, from plate 31, the projected tooth of the 30-tooth gear, to the 30-tooth gear of this drawing. Having transferred the tooth, it should be carefully compared with the original so as to be sure that the transfer has been accurately made. Being satisfied that it is correct, the remaining teeth may be drawn. The work from this point on is similar to plate 30, and should be completed without any further instructions.

The 25-tooth gear is drawn in the same manner.

PROFILES OF GEAR TEETH.

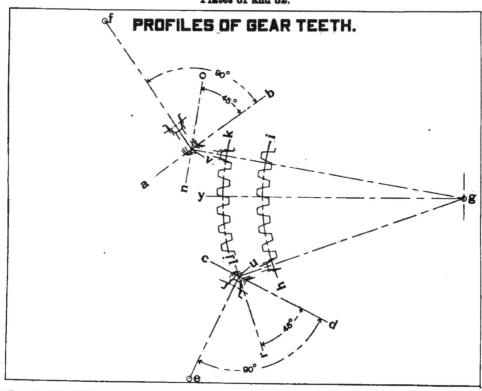

SPIRAL GEARING.

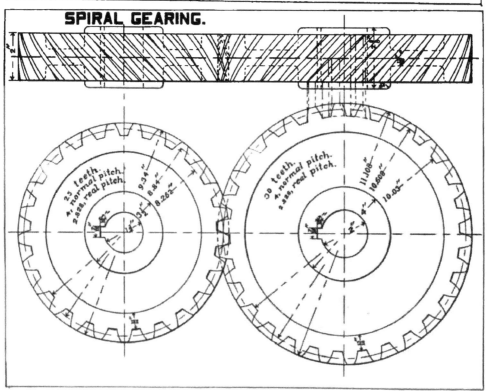

SCREW CUTTING.

Rule.—Divide the pitch of the screw to be cut, by the pitch of the lead-screw. The lead-screw, is that screw which moves the lathe-carriage along the shears of the lathe. The movement of the carriage, per revolution of the work, is regulated by gears on the end of the lathe; these gears are called change gears.

Suppose it is required to cut a screw of 4 threads per inch with a lead-screw having 5 threads per inch.

Four threads per inch is equal to $\frac{1}{4}$-inch pitch, and 5 threads per inch is equal to $\frac{1}{5}$-inch pitch; because, in the former case, the distance from the center of one thread to the center of the next is $\frac{1}{4}$ of an inch, and in the latter case, the distance from the center of one thread to the center of the next is $\frac{1}{5}$ of an inch.

$$\text{Then } \frac{1}{4} \div \frac{1}{5} = \frac{1}{4} \times \frac{5}{1} = \frac{5 \text{ gear on the stud}}{4 \text{ gear on the lead-screw}}.$$

As gears are not made with so small a number of teeth, we must raise the fraction $\frac{5}{4}$ by multiplying both terms of the fraction by some number, say 10,

$$\frac{5}{4} \times \frac{10}{10} = \frac{50 \text{ gear on the stud.}}{40 \text{ gear on the lead-screw.}}$$

If the thread to be cut is fractional, as $5\frac{1}{4}$ threads per inch; one inch must be divided by $5\frac{1}{4}$ so as to obtain the pitch of the thread, thus,

$$5\frac{1}{4} = \frac{21}{4} \text{ and } 1 \div \frac{21}{4} = 1 \times \frac{4}{21}$$

of an inch, pitch, and the pitch of the lead-screw is $\frac{1}{5}$-inch pitch, and

$$\frac{4}{21} \div \frac{1}{5} = \frac{4}{21} \times \frac{5}{1} = \frac{20 \text{ gear on the stud.}}{21 \text{ gear on the lead-screw.}}$$

Suppose we are required to cut a screw of $1\frac{5}{8}$ inches pitch; heretofore, the pitch of the thread has been a part of an inch, in this case, the pitch is greater than an inch, that is, we have one thread for every $1\frac{5}{8}$ inches. This pitch, $1\frac{5}{8}$ is equal to $\frac{13}{8}$ or, 8 threads in 13 inches. $\frac{13}{8}$ divided by the pitch of the lead-screw, equals

$$\frac{13}{8} \div \frac{1}{5} = \frac{13}{8} \times \frac{5}{1} = \frac{65 \text{ gear on the stud.}}{8 \text{ gear on the lead-screw.}}$$

Here, as in a former case, we must raise the fraction by multiplying both terms of the fraction by some number, as

$$\frac{65}{8} \times \frac{3}{3} = \frac{195 \text{ gear on the stud.}}{24 \text{ gear on the lead-screw.}}$$

NOTE.—The numerator of the fraction always denotes the number of inches, and the denominator, the number of threads in that number of inches as $\frac{1}{4}$-inch pitch is 4 threads in one inch, $\frac{4}{21}$-inch pitch is 21 threads in 4 inches, $\frac{5}{16}$-inch pitch is 16 threads in 5 inches. This is true whatever the pitch.

CAUTION.—Do not get a pitch like $1\frac{5}{8}$-inch pitch, confounded with $1\frac{5}{8}$ threads per inch, as $1\frac{5}{8}$-inch pitch is $\frac{13}{8}$ or 8 threads in 13 inches, and $1\frac{5}{8}$ threads per inch is

$$1 \div \frac{13}{8} = \frac{8}{13} \text{-inch pitch or, 13 threads in 8 inches.}$$

So far, we have only considered simple gearing, that is, the gear on the stud driving the intermediate gear, and the same intermediate driving the gear on the lead-screw.

When two or more intermediate gears are used, the gearing is said to be compound. Assume a screw of one thread in $1\frac{3}{4}$ inches. Now, $1\frac{3}{4}$ equals $\frac{7}{4}$-inch pitch, and $\frac{7}{4}$ divided by $\frac{1}{5}$-inch, pitch of the lead-screw thread, equals

$$\frac{7}{4} \div \frac{1}{5} = \frac{7}{4} \times \frac{5}{1} = \frac{35}{4}$$

The difference between the number of teeth in the large gear and the number of teeth in the small gear is too great to permit them being used as simple gearing; which makes it necessary to compound them in the following manner:

$\dfrac{35 \div 5 = 7}{4 \div 2 = 2}$ 5 and 7 are the factors of 35, and 2 and 2 are the factors of 4. Now,

multiply both terms of the fraction $\frac{5}{2}$ by some number as $\dfrac{5}{2} \times \dfrac{10}{10} = \dfrac{50}{20}$ and both

terms of the fraction $\frac{7}{2}$ by some number as $\dfrac{7}{2} \times \dfrac{8}{8} = \dfrac{56}{16}$ the gears $\dfrac{50}{20}\dfrac{56}{16}$ are equiva-

lent to, and will do the same work as $\frac{35}{4}$ and are placed on the lathe in the following manner: 50 gear on the stud.
        20 first gear on the intermediate stud.
        56 second gear on the intermediate stud.
        16 gear on the lead screw.

Or, $\frac{50}{20}$ $\frac{56}{16}$ may be arranged like this $\frac{56}{16}$ $\frac{50}{20}$ now the arrangement on the lathe will be   56 gear on the stud.
        16 first gear on the intermediate stud.
        50 second gear on the intermediate stud.
        20 gear on the lead screw.

Threads are quite frequently irregular, as $4\frac{3}{4}$ threads in $3\frac{5}{8}$ inches.

$$4\frac{3}{4} = \frac{19}{4} \text{ and } 3\frac{5}{8} = \frac{29}{8} ;$$

$\frac{29}{8}$ is the length which contains $\frac{19}{4}$ threads. The length divided by the number of threads equale pitch, as

$$\frac{29}{8} \div \frac{19}{4} = \frac{29}{8} \times \frac{4}{19} = \frac{116}{152} ;$$

as this is large, it should be reduced to lower terms, which may be done without

changing its value, as $\dfrac{116 \div 4}{152 \div 4} = \dfrac{29}{38}$ inch pitch, which, divided by the pitch of the

lead-screw will give the required gears.

Let the pitch of the lead-screw be 4 threads per inch, equals $\frac{1}{4}$-inch pitch, then

$\dfrac{29}{38} \div \dfrac{1}{4} = \dfrac{29}{38} \times \dfrac{4}{1} = \dfrac{116}{83}$ factoring we have $\dfrac{116 \div 4}{38 \div 2} = \dfrac{29}{19}$ then $\dfrac{4}{2} \times \dfrac{10}{10} = \dfrac{40}{20}$,

and $\dfrac{29}{19} \times \dfrac{2}{2} = \dfrac{58}{38}$. $\dfrac{40}{20}\dfrac{58}{38}$ are the gears. The arrangement on the lathe is:

        40 gear on the stud.
        20 first gear on the intermediate stud.
        58 second gear on the intermediate stud.
        38 gear on the lead-screw.

The intermediate stud usually has a sleeve which works freely on the stud, with a key which fits the key-seats in the change gears, and thus keeping the two intermediate gears, which are put on the sleeve, in the same relation to each other.

To prove a set of gears, divide the product of the teeth of the driven gears by the pitch of the lead-screw, then this quotient divided by the product of the teeth in the driving gears will give the number of threads per inch. Or, if there are only two gears, then the number of teeth in the gear on the lead-screw may be divided by the pitch of the lead-screw, and this quotient divided by the number of teeth in the gear on the stud will give the number of threads per inch.

Table No. 1.

20° LINE OF ACTION, CIRCULAR PITCH.

Note:—This table can be used only for 20° line of action. Multiply tabular numbers by circular pitch to obtain the different radii.

For 20° line of action ·

Radius of face curve = $.34202 \times r + (.2125\ p)$.

Radius of flank curve = $.04125 \times p \times n$.

r = radius of pitch circle.

p = circular pitch.

n = number of teeth.

Column No. 1. No. of teeth.	Column No. 2. Radius of face,	Column No. 3. Radius of flank.	Column No. 4. Radius of circle at centre.	Column No. 5. Radius of fillet.
12	86568	.495	.2	.15
13	92	.53625	.15	.15
14	.97452	.5775	.125	.125
15	1.02896	.61875	Radial	.125
16	1.1034	.66	"	.125
17	1.1378	.70125	"	.125
18	1.19224	.7425	"	.125
20	1.30114	.825	Curve	.1
22	1.41004	.9075	"	.1
24	1.5188	.99	"	.075
26	1.6277	1.0725	"	.075
30	1 8454	1.2375	"	.05
40	2.38978	1.65	"	.0375
50	2.934	2.062	"	.0375
70	4.0227	2.887	"	.0375
100	5.6557	4.125	"	.0375
150	8.3773	6.187	"	.0375
300	16.542	12.375	"	.0375
Rack				

Table No. 2.

20° LINE OF ACTION, DIAMETRAL PITCH.

Note:—This table can be used only for 20° line of action.   Divide tabular numbers by diametral pitch to obtain the radii.

Column No. 1. No. of teeth.	Column No. 2. Radius of face.	Column No. 3. Radius of flank.	Column No. 4. Radius of circle at centre.	Column No. 5. Radius of fillet.
12	2.7193	1.5551	.6283	.4712
13	2.8902	1.6845	.4722	.4712
14	3.0614	1.8142	.3927	.3927
15	3.2323	1.9437	Radial	.3927
16	3.4664	2.0734	"	.3927
17	3.5745	2.2028	"	.3927
18	3.7454	2.3326	"	.3927
20	4.0875	2.5918	Curve	.3141
22	4.4296	2.8510	"	.3141
24	4.7714	3.1100	"	.2356
26	5.1135	3.3693	"	.2356
30	5.7975	3.8877	"	.1570
40	7.5074	5.1836	"	.1178
50	9.2174	6.4779	"	.1178
70	12.6377	9.0697	"	.1178
100	17.7679	12.9591	"	.1178
150	26.3181	19.4370	"	.1178
300	51.9683	38.8773	"	.1178
Rack				

Table No. 8.

14¼° LINE OF ACTION, CIRCULAR PITCH.

Note:—This table can be used only for 14½° line of action. Multiply tabular numbers by circular pitch to obtain the different radii.

For 14½° line of action :

Radius of face curve $= .25038 \times r + (.2125 \ p)$.

Radius of flank curve $= .033 \times p \times n$.

$r =$ radius of pitch circle.

$p =$ circular pitch.

$n =$ number of teeth.

Column No. 1. No. of teeth.	Column No. 2 Radius of face.	Column No. 3. Radius of flank.	Column No. 4. Radius of circle at centre.	Column No. 5. Radius of fillet.
12	.6906	.396	.23125	.175
13	.7305	.429	.1982	.1708
14	.7703	.462	.1652	.1666
15	.8102	.495	.1321	.1625
16	.8500	.528	.0991	.1583
17	.8899	.561	.0661	.1542
18	.9297	.594	.0330	.1500
20	1.0094	.660	Radial	.1417
22	1.0891	.726	"	.1333
24	1.1688	.792	"	.1250
26	1.2485	.858	"	.1167
30	1.4079	.990	"	.1000
40	1.8064	1.320	Curve	.0583
50	2.2048	1.650	"	.0500
70	3.0018	2.310	"	.0500
100	4.1972	3.300	"	.0500
150	6.1896	4.950	"	.0500
300 Rack	6.1896	9.900	"	.0500

Table No. 4.

14½° LINE OF ACTION, DIAMETRAL PITCH.

Note:—This table can be used only for 14½° line of action   Divide tabular numbers by diametral pitch to obtain the radii.

Column No. 1. No. of teeth.	Column No. 2. Radius of face.	Column No. 3. Radius of flank.	Column No. 4. Radius of circle at centre.	Column No. 5. Radius of fillet.
12	2.1696	1.2441	.7264	.54978
13	2.2949	1.3477	.6227	.53658
14	2.4200	1.4514	.5189	.52339
15	2.5453	1.5551	.4151	.51051
16	2.6704	1.6588	.3114	.49731
17	2.7957	1.7624	.2076	.48443
18	2.9207	1.8661	.1038	.47124
20	3.1711	2.0734	Radial	.44516
22	3.4215	2.2808	"	.41877
24	3.6719	2.4881	"	.39270
26	4.0223	2.6955	"	.36662
30	4.4230	3.1102	"	.31416
40	5.6750	4.1469	Curve	.1835
50	6.9266	5.1836	"	.15708
70	9.4304	7.2571	"	.15708
100	13.1859	10.3672	"	.15708
150	19.4452	15.5509	"	.15708
300	19.4452	31.1018	"	.15708
Rack				

Table No. 5.

FRANKLIN INSTITUTE OR U. S. STANDARD BOLT AND NUT PROPORTIONS.

Diameter of Bolt.	Threads per inch.	Root Diameter = Diameter − 1.3 of Pitch.	Width of Flats = .126 of Pitch.	Width over Flats = 1.5 Diameter + 1/16".	Long Diameter = Width over Flats × 1.154.	Thickness of Head and Nut = diameter − 1/16".	Diameter of Washer = 2 Diameters + 1/16".	Thickness of Washer.
1/4"	20	.185"	.0062"	7/16"	.505"	3/16"	9/16"	3/32"
5/16"	18	.240"	.0074"	17/32"	.613"	1/4"	11/16"	1/8"
3/8"	16	.294"	.0078"	5/8"	.722"	5/16"	13/16"	1/8"
7/16"	14	.344"	.0089"	23/32"	.830"	3/8"	15/16"	5/32"
1/2"	13	.400"	.0096"	13/16"	.938"	7/16"	1 1/16"	5/32"
9/16"	12	.454"	.0104"	29/32"	1.046"	1/2"	1 3/16"	3/16"
5/8"	11	.507"	.0113"	1"	1.154"	9/16"	1 5/16"	3/16"
3/4"	10	.620"	.0125"	1 3/16"	1.371"	11/16"	1 9/16"	7/32"
7/8"	9	.731"	.0138"	1 3/8"	1.587"	13/16"	1 13/16"	7/32"
1"	8	.837"	.0156"	1 9/16"	1.804"	15/16"	2 1/16"	1/4"
1 1/8"	7	.940"	.0178"	1 3/4"	2.020"	1 1/16"	2 5/16"	1/4"
1 1/4"	7	1.065"	.0178"	1 7/8"	2.237"	1 3/16"	2 9/16"	9/32"
1 3/8"	6	1.160"	.0208"	2 1/8"	2.453"	1 5/16"	2 13/16"	9/32"
1 1/2"	6	1.284"	.0208"	2 5/16"	2.670"	1 7/16"	3 1/16"	5/16"
1 5/8"	5 1/2	1.389"	.0227"	2 1/2"	2.886"	1 9/16"	3 5/16"	5/16"
1 3/4"	5	1.491"	.0250"	2 11/16"	3.103"	1 11/16"	3 9/16"	11/32"
1 7/8"	5	1.616"	.0250"	2 7/8"	3.319"	1 13/16"	3 13/16"	1/2"
2"	4 1/2	1.712"	.0277"	3 1/16"	3.536"	1 15/16"	4 1/16"	11/32"
2 1/4"	4 1/2	1.962"	.0277"	3 7/16"	3.969"	2 3/16"	4 9/16"	3/8"
2 1/2"	4	2.176"	.0312"	3 13/16"	4.402"	2 7/16"	5 1/16"	13/32"
2 3/4"	4	2.426"	.0312"	4 3/16"	4.835"	2 11/16"	5 9/16"	7/8"
3"	3 1/2	2.629"	.0357"	4 7/8"	5.268"	2 15/16"	6 1/16"	15/16"

These are finished sizes.   Add 1/8" for rough sizes instead of 1/16"

TABLE No. 6.   TABLE No. 7.

Diametral pitch.	Equivalent circular pitch.	Circular pitch.	Equivalent diametral pitch.
2	1.5708 inch.	2 inch.	1.571
2¼	1.3962 "	1⅞ "	1.676
2½	1.2566 "	1¾ "	1.795
2¾	1.1424 "	1⅝ "	1.933
3	1.0472 "	1½ "	2.094
3½	.8976 "	1⁷⁄₁₆ "	2.185
4	.7854 "	1⅜ "	2.285
5	.6283 "	1⁵⁄₁₆ "	2.394
6	.5236 "	1¼ "	2.513
7	.4488 "	1³⁄₁₆ "	2.646
8	.3927 "	1⅛ "	2.793
9	.3491 "	1¹⁄₁₆ "	2.957
10	.3142 "	1 "	3.142
11	.2856 "	15⁄16 "	3.351
12	.2618 "	⅞ "	3.590
14	.2244 "	13⁄16 "	3.867
16	.1963 "	¾ "	4.189
18	.1745 "	11⁄16 "	4.570
20	.1571 "	⅝ "	5.027
22	.1428 "	9⁄16 "	5.585
24	.1309 "	½ "	6.283
26	.1208 "	7⁄16 "	7.181
28	.1122 "	⅜ "	8.378
30	.1047 "	5⁄16 "	10.053
32	.0982 "	¼ "	12.566
36	.0873 "	3⁄16 "	16.755
40	.0785 "	⅛ "	25.133
48	.0654 "	1⁄16 "	50.266

TABLE No. 8.

Table giving the diameter in decimals of the numbers of the twist drill and steel wire gauge.

No.	Diameter of number in decimals.	No.	Diameter of number in decimals.	No.	Diameter of number in decimals.
1	.2280	21	.1590	41	.0960
2	.2210	22	.1570	42	.0935
3	.2130	23	.1540	43	.0890
4	.2090	24	.1520	44	.0860
5	.2055	25	.1495	45	.0820
6	.2040	26	.1470	46	.0810
7	.2010	27	.1440	47	.0785
8	.1990	28	.1405	48	.0760
9	.1960	29	.1360	49	.0730
10	.1935	30	.1285	50	.0700
11	.1910	31	.1200	51	.0670
12	.1890	32	.1160	52	.0635
13	.1850	33	.1130	53	.0595
14	.1820	34	.1110	54	.0550
15	.1800	35	.1100	55	.0520
16	.1770	36	.1065	56	.0465
17	.1730	37	.1040	57	.0430
18	.1695	38	.1015	58	.0420
19	.1660	39	.0995	59	.0410
20	.1610	40	.0980	60	.0400

DECIMAL EQUIVALENTS.

8ths.

1/8	= .125
1/4	= .250
3/8	= .375
1/2	= .500
5/8	= .625
3/4	= .750
7/8	= .875

16ths.

1/16	= .0625
3/16	= .1875
5/16	= .3125
7/16	= .4375
9/16	= .5625
11/16	= .6875
13/16	= .8125
15/16	= .9375

32nds.

1/32	= .03125	7/32	= .21875
3/32	= .09375	9/32	= .28125
5/32	= .15625	11/32	= .34375
		13/32	= .40625
		15/32	= .46875
		17/32	= .53125
		19/32	= .59375
		21/32	= .65625
		23/32	= .71875
		25/32	= .78125
		27/32	= .84375
		29/32	= .90625
		31/32	= .96875

64ths.

1/64	= .015625	17/64	= .265625
3/64	= .046875	19/64	= .296875
5/64	= .078125	21/64	= .328125
7/64	= .109375	23/64	= .359375
9/64	= .140625	25/64	= .390625
11/64	= .171875	27/64	= .421875
13/64	= .203125	29/64	= .453125
15/64	= .234375	31/64	= .484375
		33/64	= .515625
		35/64	= .546875
		37/64	= .578125
		39/64	= .609375
		41/64	= .640625
		43/64	= .671875
		45/64	= .703125
		47/64	= .734375
		49/64	= .765625
		51/64	= .796875
		53/64	= .828125
		55/64	= .859375
		57/64	= .890625
		59/64	= .921875
		61/64	= .953125
		63/64	= .984375

WELDED TUBES.

Nominal inside dia.	Actual inside dia.	Actual outside dia.	Thickness of metal.	Number of thr. per inch.	Length of perfect screw.	Dia. at bottom of thr. at end of pipe.	Dia. at top of thr. at end of pipe.
1/8	0.270	0.405	0.068	27	0.19	.334	.393
1/4	0.364	0.540	0.088	18	0.29	.433	.522
3/8	0.494	0.675	0.091	18	0.30	.567	.656
1/2	0.623	0.840	0.109	14	0.39	.701	.815
3/4	0.824	1.050	0.113	14	0.40	.911	1.025
1	1.048	1.315	0.134	11½	0.51	1.144	1.283
1¼	1.380	1.660	0.140	11½	0.54	1.488	1.627
1½	1.610	1.900	0.145	11½	0.55	1.727	1.866
2	2.067	2.375	0.154	11½	0.58	2.200	2.339
2½	2.468	2.875	0.204	8	0.89	2.620	2.820
3	3.067	3.500	0.217	8	0.95	3.241	3.441
3½	3.548	4.000	0.226	8	1.00	3.738	3.938
4	4.026	4.500	0.237	8	1.05	4.235	4.435
4½	4.508	5.000	0.246	8	1.10	4.732	4.932
5	5.045	5.563	0.259	8	1.16	5.291	5.491
6	6.065	6.625	0.280	8	1.26	6.346	6.546
7	7.023	7.625	0.301	8	1.36	7.340	7.540
8	7.982	8.625	0.322	8	1.46	8.334	8.534
9	9.000	9.688	0.344	8	1.57	9.390	9.590
10	10.019	10.750	0.366	8	1.68	10.445	10.645

89083916437

This book may be kept

www.ingramcontent.com/pod-product-compliance
Lightning Source LLC
Chambersburg PA
CBHW060455060326
40689CB00020B/4539